The DK Art School

# AN INTRODUCTION TO
# DRAWING

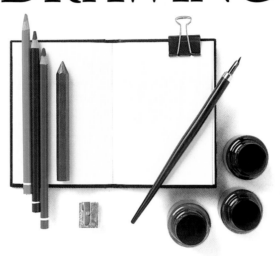

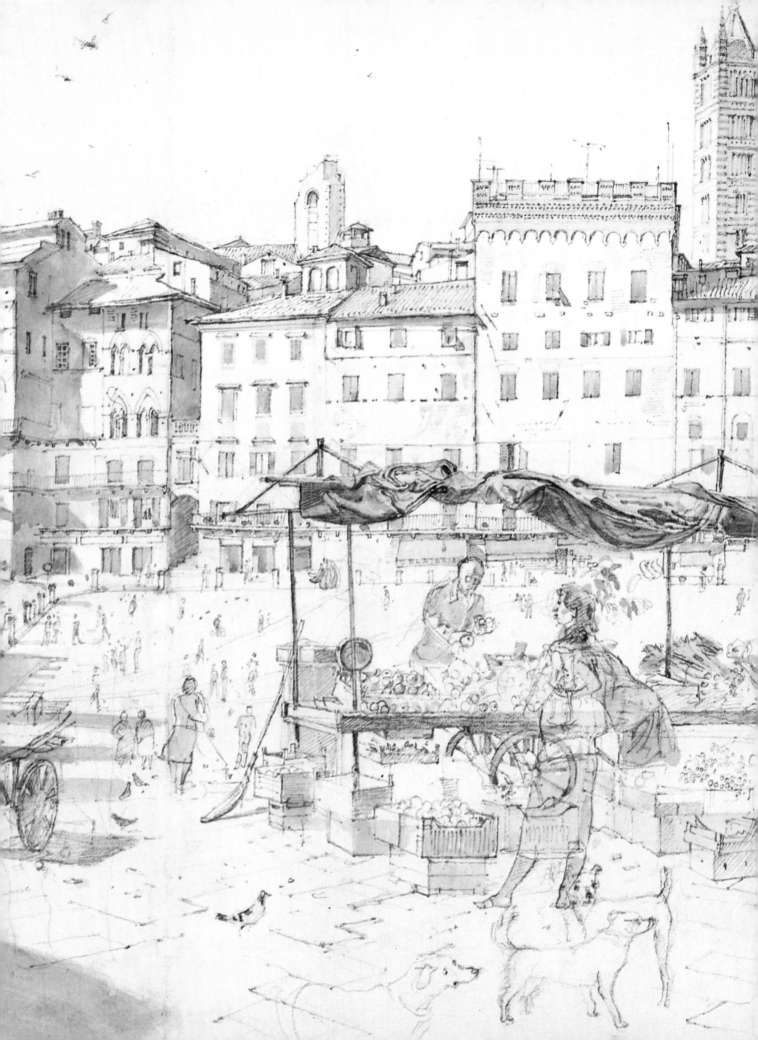

The **DK** Art School

# AN INTRODUCTION TO
# DRAWING

## JAMES HORTON

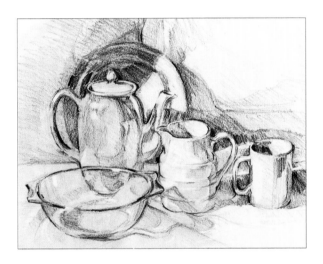

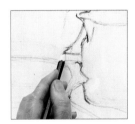 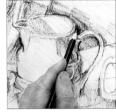 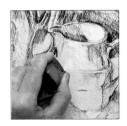 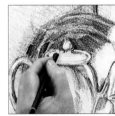

IN ASSOCIATION WITH THE ROYAL ACADEMY OF ARTS

LONDON, NEW YORK, MUNICH,
MELBOURNE, DELHI

**Project editor** Susannah Steel
**Art editor** Heather McCarry
**Designer** Dawn Terrey
**Assistant editor** Margaret Chang
**Series editor** Emma Foa
**US editors** Julee Binder,
Mary Ann Lynch, Laaren Brown
**DTP designer** Zirrinia Austin
**Managing editor** Sean Moore
**Managing art editor** Toni Kay
**Production controller** Helen Creeke
**Photography** Steve Gorton

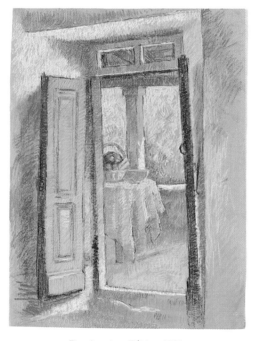

First American Edition, 1994
4 6 8 10 9 7 5

Published in the United States by DK Publishing, Inc.
375 Hudson Street New York, NY 10014

Copyright © 1994
Dorling Kindersley Limited, London

www.dk.com

Published in Great Britain by Dorling Kindersley Limited.
Distributed by Houghton Mifflin Company, Boston.

ISBN 0 7894 3288 9 PB
First paperback edition 1998

Library of Congress Cataloging-in-Publication Data
Horton, James.
    An introduction to drawing / James Horton. -- 1st American ed.
        p.    cm. -- (The DK Art School)
    Includes index.
    ISBN 1-56458-489-5
    1. Drawing--Technique.   2. Drawing materials.    I. Title.
    II. Series.
NC730.H58  1994
    741.2--dc20                                              93-34266
                                                                 CIP

Printed in China by Toppan Printing Co.,
(Shenzhen) Ltd.

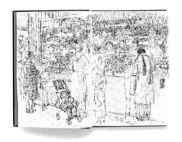

# CONTENTS

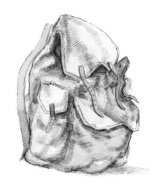

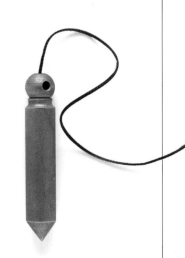

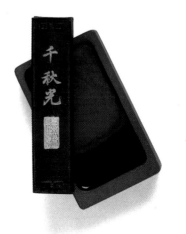

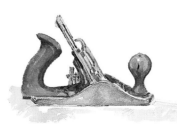

# DRAWING

AS CHILDREN WE ALL DRAW and paint – yet the older we become, the more we seem to ignore the significance of drawing as a vital source of communication and pleasure. Drawing is still one of the best ways to convey information directly, despite the increasing prevalence of photography. Scientists, and in particular archaeologists, actually prefer to draw many items because a detailed drawing can be more precise and informative than a photograph, since it involves a process of selection. Many natural history field guides rely on detailed drawings and paintings for identification purposes.

## The best approach

As adults we see the world in a very different way than children do. The stumbling block for many of us is that with a more mature perspective we have a much greater sense of what is "correct" and what is "incorrect," (although this sense limits creativity and leads us astray), and this can often create inhibitions. There is, however, nothing that is intrinsically mysterious about the mechanics of drawing. Anyone can learn to draw if they adopt the right approach. Just as with any other subject, practice is essential for achieving good results.

*Drawing well is all about how you perceive the world around you and interpret it into your own personal vision.*

## Interpreting what you see

Ultimately, drawing has far more to do with learning to see perceptively than with acquiring consummate skill with your hand. The quality of what you draw on paper stems from your imagination and the way you choose to interpret what you see. Look discerningly at objects, consolidating all the information you see, to give your drawings freshness and individuality. Don't be afraid to repeat lines or marks until a drawing looks right;

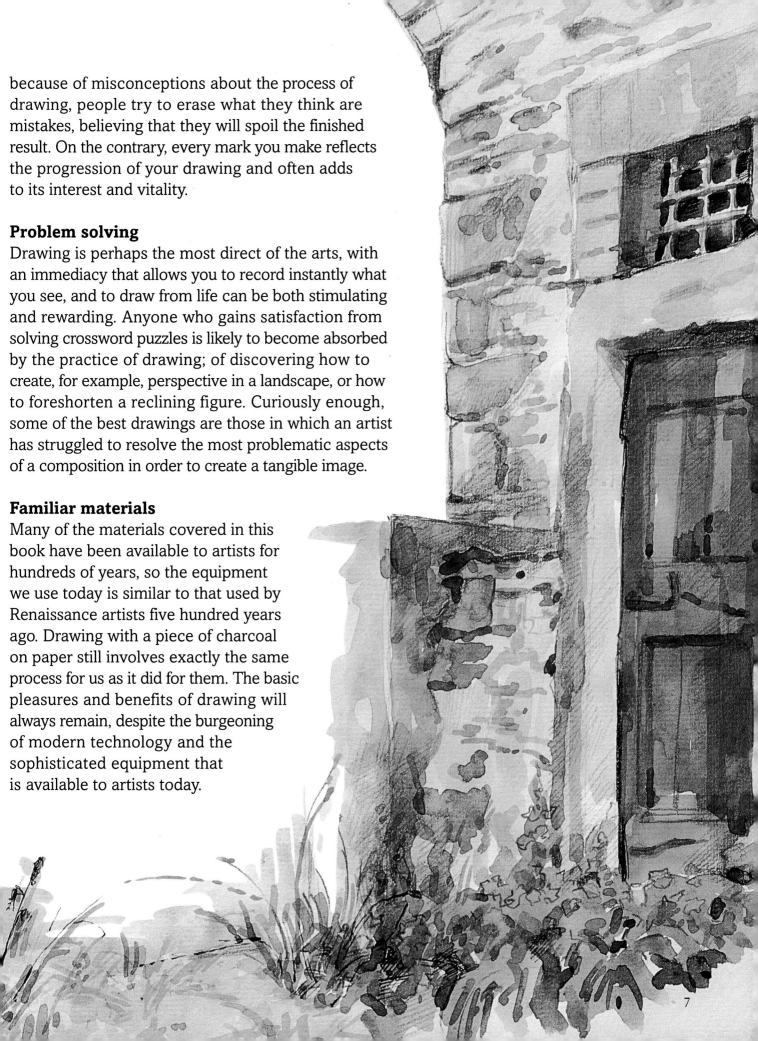

because of misconceptions about the process of drawing, people try to erase what they think are mistakes, believing that they will spoil the finished result. On the contrary, every mark you make reflects the progression of your drawing and often adds to its interest and vitality.

## Problem solving

Drawing is perhaps the most direct of the arts, with an immediacy that allows you to record instantly what you see, and to draw from life can be both stimulating and rewarding. Anyone who gains satisfaction from solving crossword puzzles is likely to become absorbed by the practice of drawing; of discovering how to create, for example, perspective in a landscape, or how to foreshorten a reclining figure. Curiously enough, some of the best drawings are those in which an artist has struggled to resolve the most problematic aspects of a composition in order to create a tangible image.

## Familiar materials

Many of the materials covered in this book have been available to artists for hundreds of years, so the equipment we use today is similar to that used by Renaissance artists five hundred years ago. Drawing with a piece of charcoal on paper still involves exactly the same process for us as it did for them. The basic pleasures and benefits of drawing will always remain, despite the burgeoning of modern technology and the sophisticated equipment that is available to artists today.

# A BRIEF HISTORY

THE HISTORY OF DRAWING may be as old as the human race itself. Cave paintings have been discovered dating back as far as 10,000 years BC, so it seems that we have always been interested in creating images. However, it was during the Italian Renaissance that artists developed profound drawing skills and the art of drawing underpinned all other artistic disciplines.

ONE REASON WHY drawing reached such a high standard during this period was that it related directly to the great profession of painting; a sculptor or a painter had a distinguished position within society and good artists were constantly working. Renaissance artists such as Michelangelo *(1475-1564)* employed numerous assistants and ran a large workshop to cope with his many commissions. Unfortunately, most of the preparatory drawings these artists made for paintings – which today we would regard as important in their own right – were destroyed once the project had been completed.

More importantly, finished drawings were presented to clients as proposals for commissioned portrait work. Holbein *(1497/8-1543)* once had the precarious task of making a suitable drawing of a potential wife for Henry VIII so that she could be approved by the English king.

### Northern Europe

Away from the high classical art of Italy, the Flemish painter Pieter Bruegel *(1525-69)* used drawing to depict the everyday world around him, and his realistic peasant scenes brought him great admiration. Bruegel was one of many artists in Holland and Flanders during the sixteenth and seventeenth centuries who cultivated a genre that was based upon the lives of ordinary people. Although this "Golden Age" of Dutch painting owed little to Italy,

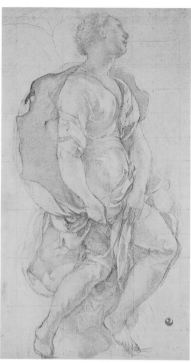

**Pontormo,**
***Study for the Angel of the Annunciation,***
**c. 1525-30** *154 x 84 in (391 x 215 cm)*
*Pontormo is generally acknowledged as one of the greatest Renaissance draftsmen and was highly regarded for his portraits. This study, with its subtle blend of chalk and wash, has a beautifully sensitive quality despite the solid form of the figure and the flowing drapery that tumbles about him.*

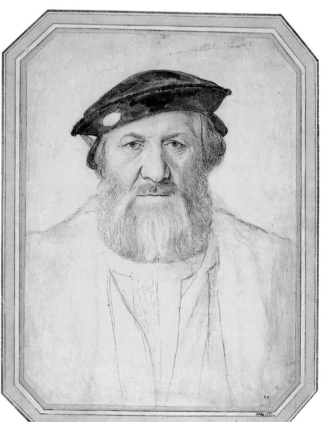

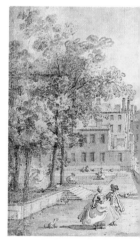

**Hans Holbein,**
***Charles de Solier,***
***Sieur de Morette,***
**c. 1534-35**
*13 x 10 in (33 x 25 cm)*
*Holbein was often commissioned to do life-like portraits. His fine quality of line both flatters the features of this figure and lends him a heavy sense of authority.*

an artist's training was based on figure drawing, which ultimately meant a pilgrimage to Italy.

One Dutch artist who never journeyed to Italy was Rembrandt *(1606-69),* who today is known particularly for his graphic work on paper. As a portrait artist, he avidly drew anyone who interested him, from old beggars to noblemen, with astonishing perception – often in his favorite medium of quill, brush, and bistre wash (a transparent brown pigment made from soot).

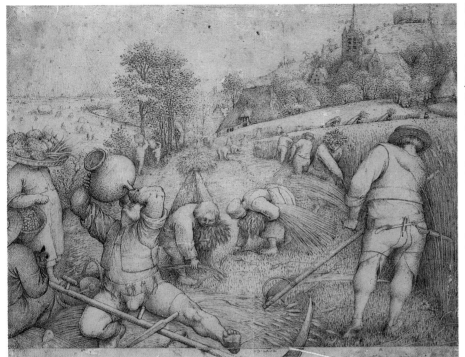

**Pieter Bruegel the Elder,**
***Summer,*** **1568** *8½ x 11½ in (22 x 29 cm)*
*This beautifully drawn study of peasant life in 16th-century Flanders is actually rather formal in its design, with the scythes of the two main figures creating diagonals that lead the eye into the middle and far distance of the composition. Bruegel also liked to convey a strong social message in his humorous depictions of life.*

## Artistic contemporaries

Rembrandt's great artistic contemporary in neighboring Flanders was Rubens *(1577-1640)*. As a draftsman, he was virtually unparalleled and was one of the few artists who appeared to make the process of drawing look easy. He drew copiously, working not only on preparatory studies for the vast number of commissions he fulfilled, but also on a much more intimate scale, depicting his family and servants with the freshness and immediacy that drawing allows.

Curiously, some of the greatest figures of the seventeenth century, such as Vermeer *(1632-75)*, Caravaggio *(1571-1610)*, and Velazquez *(1599-1660)*, left few if any drawings. Although it is improbable that these artists never drew at all, it is more likely that they preferred to solve their problems directly on the canvas in a painterly fashion.

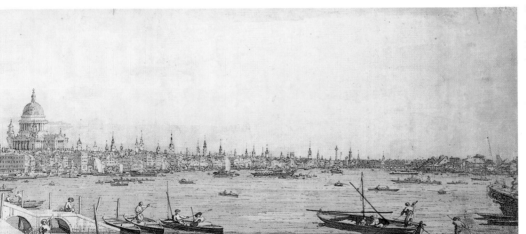

**Canaletto,** *A View from Somerset Gardens Looking Toward London Bridge, c.* **1750** *23½ x 73 in (60 x 185 cm)*
*Canaletto was renowned for his detailed paintings and drawings of architectural scenes. The wonderful clarity of this work was achieved by drawing the panoramic composition in pencil and then overlaying it with brown ink and gray wash.*

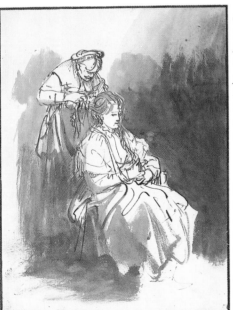

**Rembrandt,** *Saskia at her Toilet,*
**c.** **1632-34** *9½ x 7 in (24 x 18 cm)*
*Rembrandt was often at his best when he recorded a fleeting moment in time. This drawing reflects the precision of his observant eye as he worked adeptly, first with pen and ink, and then with a loaded brush. The result is a drawing that is both lucid and evocative in its depiction of a domestic scene.*

## Portrait drawing

While it did not produce many artistic giants, the eighteenth century did keep the commissioned portrait alive. In France, Watteau *(1684-1721)* produced fine studies of figures, heads, and drapery in his preferred medium of red, black, and white chalks, while in Italy, Giambattista Tiepolo *(1696-1770)*, arguably the greatest artist of his time, used pen and wash for drawings that remain unrivaled to this day.

9

## Pencil drawings

The nineteenth century saw a great surge in artistic development, which in England began with Turner *(1775-1851)* and Constable *(1776-1837),* and in France with Delacroix *(1798-1863)* and Ingres *(1780-1867).* Lead pencil was in use by this time, and Constable used the medium to draw many small images of rural Suffolk in his sketchbooks with great subtlety and expression. Turner began to develop almost unbelievable powers of observation and skill in his youth as he drew cathedrals and buildings with a lead pencil.

Portrait drawings were still fashionable, and studies drawn by the French Neo-Classicist Ingres were so real and lifelike that there was never any doubt as to their likeness to the sitter. Ingres' contemporary and great rival was Delacroix, who by contrast was a Romantic free spirit. He not only made studies in the traditional manner for grand historical pictures but also drew everything that caught his eye. In an age that preceded the advent of photography, drawing was the only way that Delacroix could record the trip he made to Morocco in 1832. Contemporary reports stated that he drew night and day, desperate not to forget the rich aspects of Arabian life.

## The advent of modernity

Of the great draftsmen of the nineteenth century, one innovative artist assimilated everything that went before him. This was Edgar Degas *(1834-1917),* whose life's work was based on drawing. Even as a middle-aged and well-established artist, he copied works by other artists to stretch his understanding of art and practice his techniques. Degas' enormous output of drawings, pastels, monoprints, and etchings represents an incredible achievement, but by the time he died in 1917, the modern art

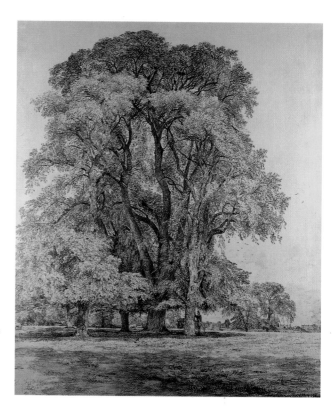

**John Constable, *Elm Trees in Old Hall Park, East Bergholt,* 1817**
*23¼ x 19½ in (59 x 50 cm)*
*Unlike Turner, who used a wide variety of media in his drawings, Constable preferred to use his materials separately to describe the countryside around him. He used a pencil expertly to capture the organic growth of these elm trees with incredible detail so that they are easily recognizable.*

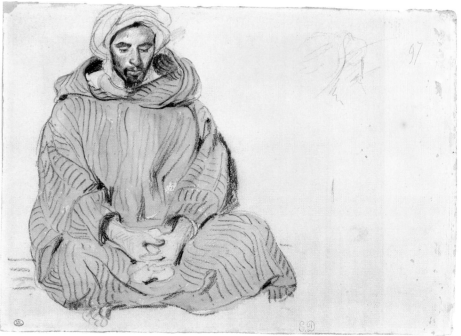

**Eugène Delacroix, *Seated Arab,* c. 1832** *15 x 18 in (38 x 46 cm)*
*This study is typical of the sketches Delacroix made during his Moroccan tour. He probably drew the figure hastily from life and added washes of watercolor later.*

movement was well under way and moving rapidly toward a language that he would not have recognized.

The history of drawing from this point is a checkered one, and it developed quite differently on the two sides of the English Channel. While France pursued modernism, spurred on by artists such as Henri Matisse *(1869-1954),* England retained a basic attachment to drawing. The turn of the century in England saw the birth of several major art schools, all of which placed a great emphasis on drawing, and although

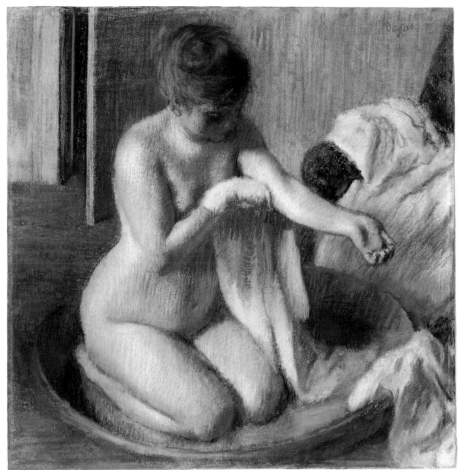

various modern movements came and went, drawing continued to underpin students' training. The work of artists such as Augustus John *(1878-1961)* and later Stanley Spencer *(1891-1959)* bear witness to the significance of drawing in England through the turbulent years of the early twentieth century.

One artist who has brought drawing to the forefront of the contemporary imagination is David Hockney *(b.1937)*. Inspired by Pablo Picasso *(1881-1973)*, who had an extraordinary breadth of style and "was not limited by 'form,'" Hockney takes pleasure in the lyricism and strength of pure line. Preferring the expressive beauty of drawings over more painterly approaches, Hockney has taken his drawing to a far wider audience than ever before.

**Edgar Degas,** *Woman in a Tub,*
*c.* **1885** *27½ x 27½ in (70 x 70 cm)*
*Classically trained, Degas devised his own method of working with pastels. He built them up in layers, using strokes of color that blended optically to give an extraordinary richness.*

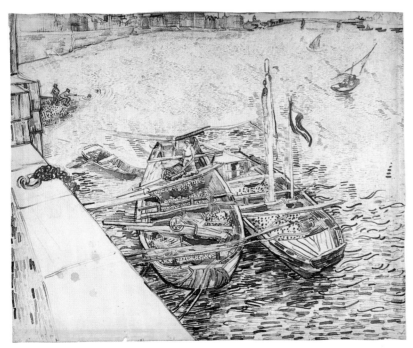

**Vincent van Gogh,** *Sand Boats,*
**1888** *19 x 23½ in (49 x 60 cm)*
*Van Gogh exploited the potential of pen and ink to its fullest in this work to produce an image alive with spontaneous line. A variety of marks and stippled effects together create a*
*shimmering surface of movement that is heightened by the dynamic composition. The strong diagonal of the quayside and the horizon line that cuts into the top of the drawing create an arena for this scene of constant activity and motion.*

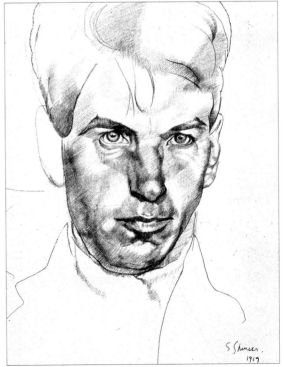

**Stanley Spencer,** *Self-Portrait,*
**1919** *14 x 9 in (36 x 23 cm)*
*The strong contours and subtle tones of this pencil study lend it an impressive sculpted quality. The solidity of line and sensitive tones belie the apparent simplicity of the medium.*

11

# PENCILS & COLORED PENCILS

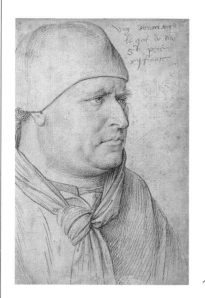

**P**ENCILS ARE THE SIMPLEST and most immediate of drawing media, enabling you to create a versatile range of strong or sensitive marks. What we call a "lead pencil" today is actually made of graphite – a mixture of clay and the mineral graphite – in the form of a rod that is usually encased in cedarwood. An array of grades exists from very hard to extremely soft, although artists seldom use the hardest varieties because they allow for so little expression when drawing. Colored pencils are a relatively recent innovation, and their waxy nature means that they retain their own distinct colors when drawn over each other.

**Silverpoint study**
*Silverpoint, an original version of the pencil popular in Renaissance times, is a beautiful medium, as this 15th century study by Fouquet shows. The basic principle of silverpoint is to leave a metal deposit by dragging a piece of pure silver across paper previously prepared with Chinese White watercolor paint.*

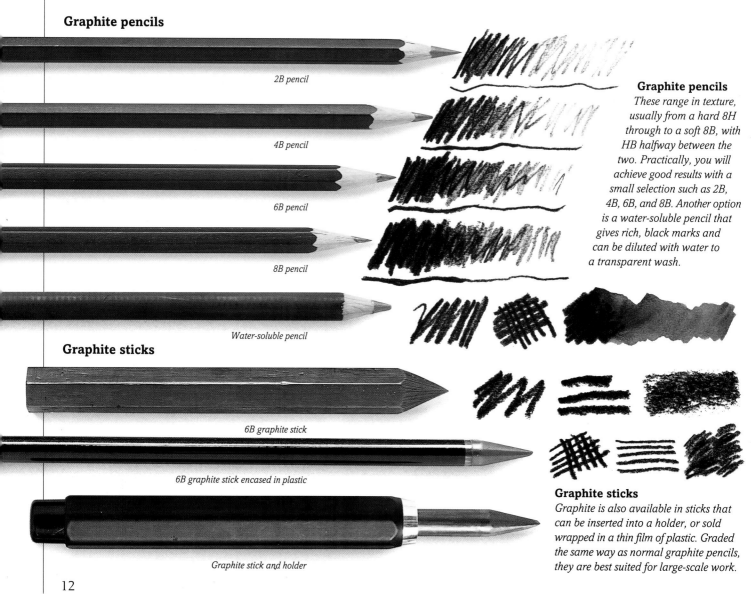

**Graphite pencils**

*2B pencil*

*4B pencil*

*6B pencil*

*8B pencil*

*Water-soluble pencil*

**Graphite pencils**
*These range in texture, usually from a hard 8H through to a soft 8B, with HB halfway between the two. Practically, you will achieve good results with a small selection such as 2B, 4B, 6B, and 8B. Another option is a water-soluble pencil that gives rich, black marks and can be diluted with water to a transparent wash.*

**Graphite sticks**

*6B graphite stick*

*6B graphite stick encased in plastic*

*Graphite stick and holder*

**Graphite sticks**
*Graphite is also available in sticks that can be inserted into a holder, or sold wrapped in a thin film of plastic. Graded the same way as normal graphite pencils, they are best suited for large-scale work.*

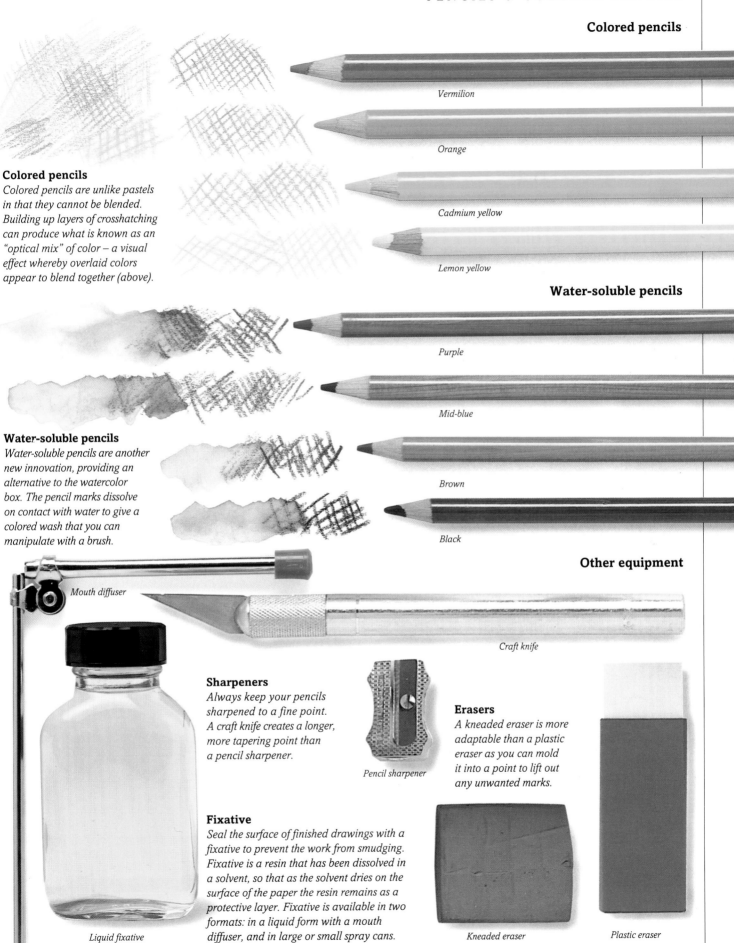

## Colored pencils

**Vermilion**

**Orange**

**Cadmium yellow**

**Lemon yellow**

### Colored pencils
*Colored pencils are unlike pastels in that they cannot be blended. Building up layers of crosshatching can produce what is known as an "optical mix" of color – a visual effect whereby overlaid colors appear to blend together (above).*

## Water-soluble pencils

**Purple**

**Mid-blue**

**Brown**

**Black**

### Water-soluble pencils
*Water-soluble pencils are another new innovation, providing an alternative to the watercolor box. The pencil marks dissolve on contact with water to give a colored wash that you can manipulate with a brush.*

## Other equipment

*Mouth diffuser*

*Craft knife*

### Sharpeners
*Always keep your pencils sharpened to a fine point. A craft knife creates a longer, more tapering point than a pencil sharpener.*

*Pencil sharpener*

### Erasers
*A kneaded eraser is more adaptable than a plastic eraser as you can mold it into a point to lift out any unwanted marks.*

### Fixative
*Seal the surface of finished drawings with a fixative to prevent the work from smudging. Fixative is a resin that has been dissolved in a solvent, so that as the solvent dries on the surface of the paper the resin remains as a protective layer. Fixative is available in two formats: in a liquid form with a mouth diffuser, and in large or small spray cans.*

*Liquid fixative*

*Kneaded eraser*

*Plastic eraser*

13

# PENS & INKS

PEN AND INK has been for centuries one of the most common drawing mediums. In the past, pens were almost always made from quills, although reeds and bamboo were also used. Today, there is an abundance of pens to choose from, many of which can be used by artists, although the quality of ink in most commercially available pens is often poor and will fade over time. Drawing in ink is always a great challenge because the ink is impossible to erase and so, in many senses, embodies the spirit of drawing. Every mark made becomes a vital part of the evolution of a drawing and mistakes can often be used in a constructive and interesting way.

**Quill pen**
*Traditionally made from goose feathers, the quill pen is still hard to beat in terms of flexibility and versatility. Each quill will vary in performance, depending on the strength and resistance of the shaft.*

### Choosing a pen

With so many different pens available, the only way to be sure of what suits your style is to test a random selection. A standard nib holder will take a variety of different width nibs, all of which give a variation of line depending upon the degree of pressure you exert. On the other hand, technical drawing pens, which also come in a range of sizes, are hard and inflexible and give a consistent width of line, regardless of pressure. Fountain pens are more convenient and give a good variety of line.

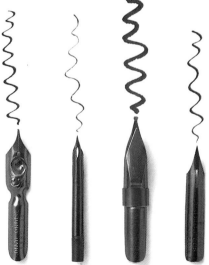

MAKING A NIB

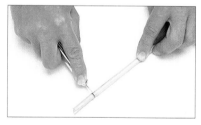

1 *Reeds, bamboo, and goose feathers are all suitable to be made into nibs. Use a craft knife to cut cleanly through one end of a reed.*

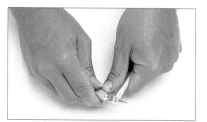

2 *Cut a curved section out of the back and trim the front into a point with two 45° angle cuts. Make a small cut to split the nib.*

**Reed pen**
*The common reed (Phragmites) is normally used to make reed pens and, like quill pens, each makes its own distinctive marks. Pens made from natural fibers need a lengthways split in the tip of the nib to act as a channel to hold the ink.*

Italic nib    Mapping nib    Script nib    Drawing nib

**Dip pens**
*Steel nibs all respond well to pressure to give a thicker or thinner line. Standard penholders take most nibs, but tubular mapping nibs need a separate holder.*

**Sketch pen**
*This pen has a flexible steel nib in a fountain pen format.*

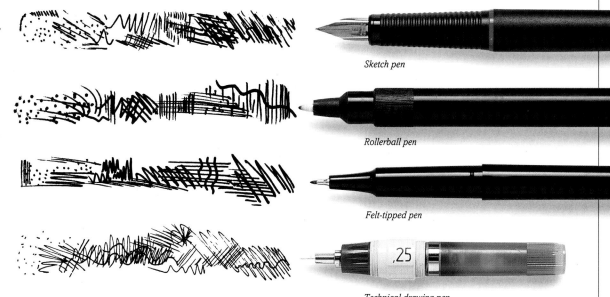

*Sketch pen*

**Rollerball pen**
*Rollerball pens act like ballpoint pens to give a steady ink flow.*

*Rollerball pen*

**Felt-tipped pen**
*A felt tip allows the ink to flow smoothly in a thin line.*

*Felt-tipped pen*

**Technical pen**
*This pen gives both good control and consistency of line.*

*Technical drawing pen*

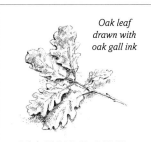

*Chinese brush*

**Chinese ink**
*Use a Chinese brush and ink block (left) for eloquent yet controlled drawings.*

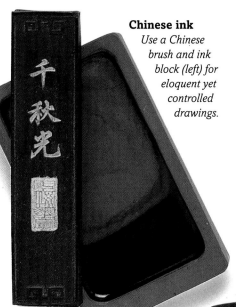

*Chinese ink*

## Using the right ink

Of the two basic types of ink – non-waterproof and waterproof – most non-waterproof inks will eventually fade if exposed to light. You can easily test for fading by drawing some lines in different inks on a piece of paper and then covering one half and leaving the other exposed to the light for several months.

*Oak leaf drawn with oak gall ink*

### MAKING INK

You can make a permanent sepia ink with oak galls from oak trees. Crush the balls and boil the powder in water for two or three hours until the liquid is dark enough to strain.

**Colored inks**
*Of the colored inks you can buy, the most common colors for drawing are black and a range of browns. In the past, ink was usually made with ground lampblack, or red ochre and a solution of glue or gum, molded into dry sticks or blocks to be mixed with water. Prepared in a similar way, India ink is a mixture of carbon black and water, stabilized by an alkaline solution such as gum arabic or shellac (a resinous substance used for making varnish).*

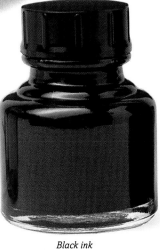

*Black ink*

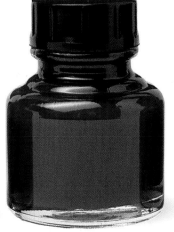

*Sepia ink*

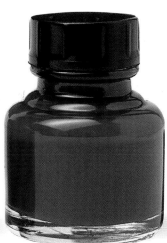

*Raw Sienna ink*

15

# CHALKS & CHARCOAL

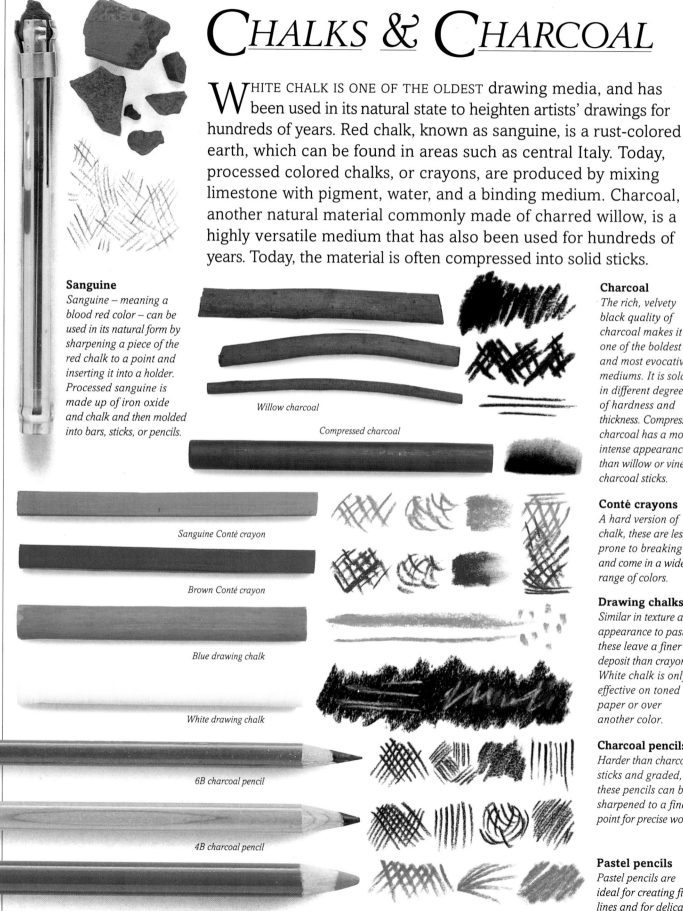

WHITE CHALK IS ONE OF THE OLDEST drawing media, and has been used in its natural state to heighten artists' drawings for hundreds of years. Red chalk, known as sanguine, is a rust-colored earth, which can be found in areas such as central Italy. Today, processed colored chalks, or crayons, are produced by mixing limestone with pigment, water, and a binding medium. Charcoal, another natural material commonly made of charred willow, is a highly versatile medium that has also been used for hundreds of years. Today, the material is often compressed into solid sticks.

**Sanguine**
*Sanguine – meaning a blood red color – can be used in its natural form by sharpening a piece of the red chalk to a point and inserting it into a holder. Processed sanguine is made up of iron oxide and chalk and then molded into bars, sticks, or pencils.*

*Willow charcoal*

*Compressed charcoal*

*Sanguine Conté crayon*

*Brown Conté crayon*

*Blue drawing chalk*

*White drawing chalk*

*6B charcoal pencil*

*4B charcoal pencil*

*Sanguine pastel pencil*

**Charcoal**
*The rich, velvety black quality of charcoal makes it one of the boldest and most evocative mediums. It is sold in different degrees of hardness and thickness. Compressed charcoal has a more intense appearance than willow or vine charcoal sticks.*

**Conté crayons**
*A hard version of chalk, these are less prone to breaking and come in a wide range of colors.*

**Drawing chalks**
*Similar in texture and appearance to pastels, these leave a finer deposit than crayons. White chalk is only effective on toned paper or over another color.*

**Charcoal pencils**
*Harder than charcoal sticks and graded, these pencils can be sharpened to a fine point for precise work.*

**Pastel pencils**
*Pastel pencils are ideal for creating fine lines and for delicate blending.*

## Drawing with Conté crayon

Conté crayons are a hard version of chalk, mixed with pigment and graphite and bound with gum and a small amount of grease. Their composition makes them harder to rub out than chalk or charcoal, so it is difficult to erase any accidental lines. They do, however, react in the same way as chalk when mixed with water; the pigment loosens on the paper so that it acts like a wash. Use a textured paper so that the distinctive qualities of Conté crayon will be heightened.

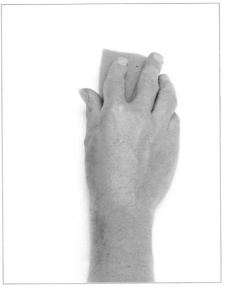

1 ▲ Begin by wetting a large sheet of paper with a household sponge. This damp surface will cause the crayon marks to absorb some of the water and appear thicker and heavier, giving a sense of solidity to the image of the figure.

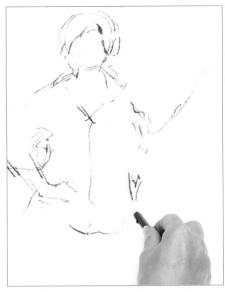

2 ▲ Draw the outlines of the standing figure with a brown Conté crayon, sketching lightly at first and then reinforcing the lines once you are happy with the proportions. Don't worry about repeating lines if you need to alter a feature.

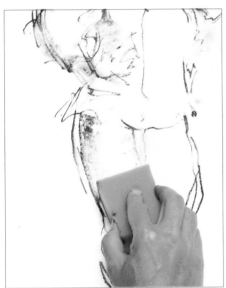

3 ▲ Now use the damp sponge to loosen the pigment in the lines of crayon. The pigment should disperse into a light wash that gives the figure a sense of shape.

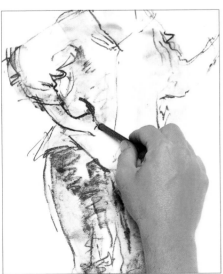

4 ◀ Use the tip of the crayon to illustrate the dark creases of the shirt and add details such as the fingers on the girl's hand.

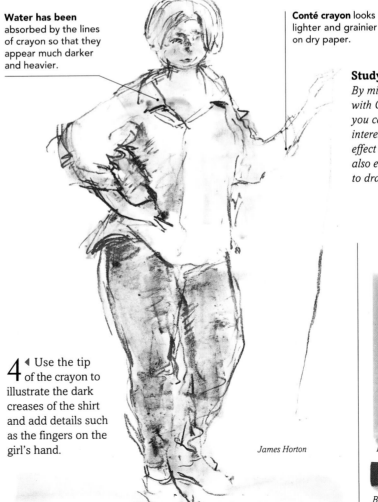

**Water has been** absorbed by the lines of crayon so that they appear much darker and heavier.

**Conté crayon** looks lighter and grainier on dry paper.

**Study of a Girl**
*By mixing water with Conté crayon you can achieve an interesting drawing effect that should also encourage you to draw lucidly.*

*James Horton*

**Materials**

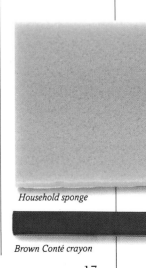

*Household sponge*

*Brown Conté crayon*

# PASTEL TYPES

THE OPAQUE NATURE of soft pastels, and their ability to cover a surface easily, means that the medium may often be used in a paintlike fashion. However, pastels cannot be mixed in the same way that paint can, so they remain within the realm of drawing – that is, the artist must use the dry sticks of pigment individually to make a series of marks, which are then overlaid or blended. Pastels are essentially chalk that has been mixed with pigment and a binding medium. They vary in hardness depending on the particular pigments and the proportion of gum to chalk. The harder they are, the better suited they are to linear work.

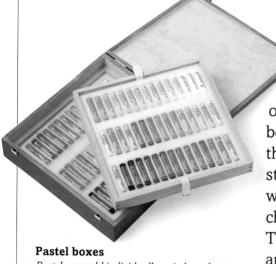

**Pastel boxes**
*Pastels are sold individually or in boxed sets that keep the colors clean and protect them.*

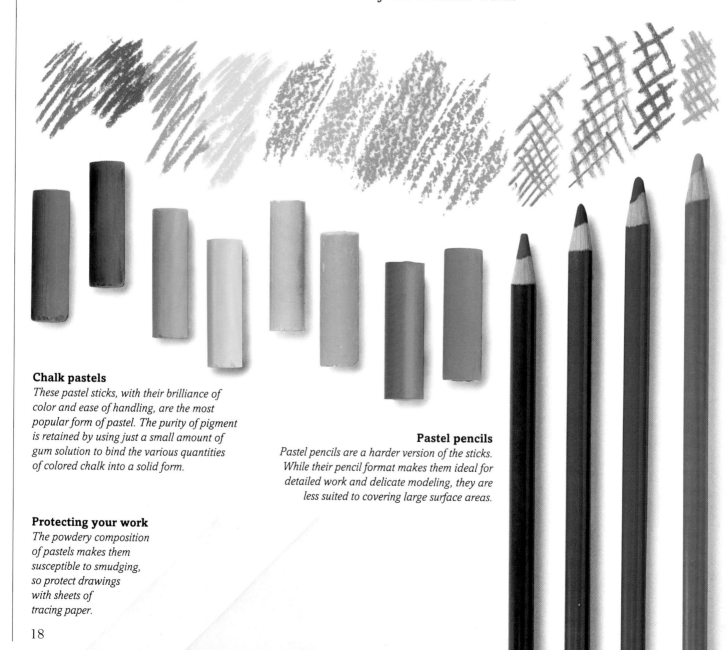

**Chalk pastels**
*These pastel sticks, with their brilliance of color and ease of handling, are the most popular form of pastel. The purity of pigment is retained by using just a small amount of gum solution to bind the various quantities of colored chalk into a solid form.*

**Pastel pencils**
*Pastel pencils are a harder version of the sticks. While their pencil format makes them ideal for detailed work and delicate modeling, they are less suited to covering large surface areas.*

**Protecting your work**
*The powdery composition of pastels makes them susceptible to smudging, so protect drawings with sheets of tracing paper.*

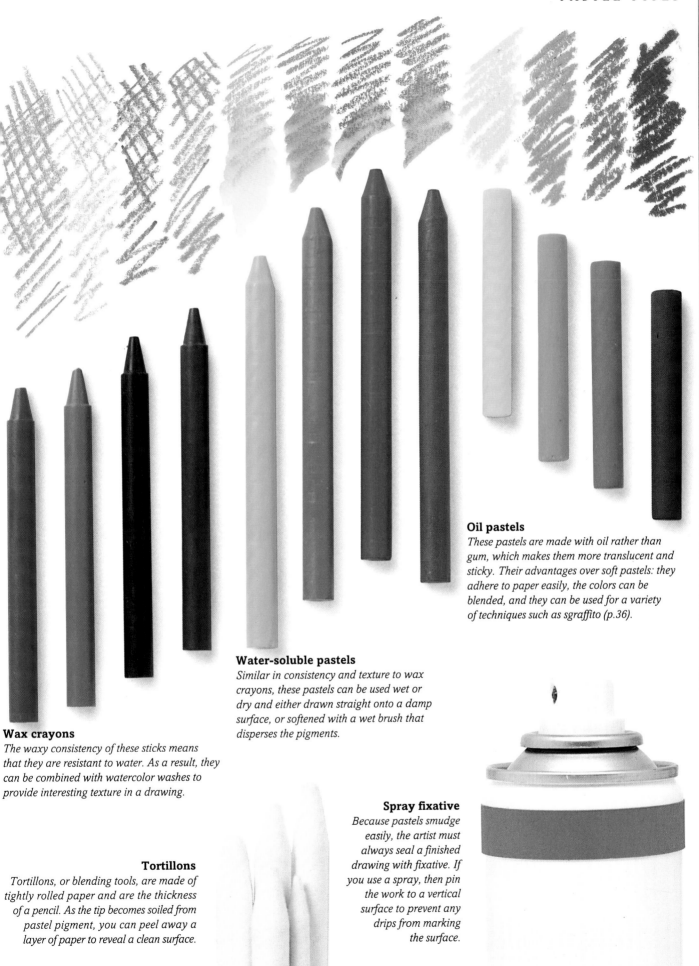

## Oil pastels
These pastels are made with oil rather than gum, which makes them more translucent and sticky. Their advantages over soft pastels: they adhere to paper easily, the colors can be blended, and they can be used for a variety of techniques such as sgraffito (p.36).

## Water-soluble pastels
Similar in consistency and texture to wax crayons, these pastels can be used wet or dry and either drawn straight onto a damp surface, or softened with a wet brush that disperses the pigments.

## Wax crayons
The waxy consistency of these sticks means that they are resistant to water. As a result, they can be combined with watercolor washes to provide interesting texture in a drawing.

## Spray fixative
Because pastels smudge easily, the artist must always seal a finished drawing with fixative. If you use a spray, then pin the work to a vertical surface to prevent any drips from marking the surface.

## Tortillons
Tortillons, or blending tools, are made of tightly rolled paper and are the thickness of a pencil. As the tip becomes soiled from pastel pigment, you can peel away a layer of paper to reveal a clean surface.

# Watercolor

Used initially in the west to "color" pen and ink drawings and heighten their descriptive qualities, watercolor has been a part of drawing media for hundreds of years. It mixes perfectly with traditional drawing tools such as pencil and ink, furnishing a linear drawing with an expressive rhythm and a pronounced spontaneity. Make sure you use permanent ink with watercolor washes or the water will dissolve the lines of ink. Watercolor is also useful because it can be blended into a smooth gradation of tones that increase the three-dimensional quality of forms in a subtle way. Using a sable brush also enables you to make the most sensuous of watercolor drawings; sable brushes offer the artist the flexibility to change instantly from a broad, bold brushmark to a fine, tapering line.

*No. 4 sable brush*

*No. 9 sable brush*

*Watercolor box*

**Transparent watercolor**
*You can blend colors together or overlay separate washes.*

**Transparency and opacity**
Watercolor is unique for its transparent light effects. The characteristic luminosity of the medium is caused by natural light penetrating a mix of pigment and water and reflecting back off the surface of the paper (*left*). The more colors you mix together, the less light can penetrate and reflect, creating a much darker color. You can also create stronger, heavier effects by mixing white with a color, or by using a watercolor paint known as gouache or body color. The opacity of gouache paint helps give solidity to an image (*below*) or create intense highlights if you are drawing on toned paper.

**Watercolor boxes**
*Watercolor paint is available in a viscous form, in a tube, or in a solid block, called a pan. Pans are most convenient for drawing as they can easily be used and stored in a metal box. Pans are sold individually so that you can replace particular colors as they run out.*

**Sable brushes**
*Soft sable brushes give the best effects with watercolor, retaining their shape far longer than synthetic brushes. A small and a medium-sized or large brush are all you need for most drawings.*

**Opaque watercolor**
*Build up dark washes of color to create strong shadows.*

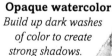

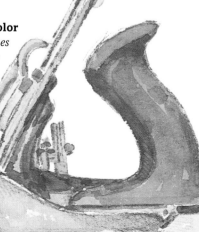

*Watercolor sketchbook*

## Working outdoors

Drawing with watercolor is almost synonymous with working outdoors or from life, because its fluency and ease of handling enable you to capture even the most fleeting of light effects. If you do decide to work outside, you can organize a simple travel kit of basic materials that takes up little room and is easy to handle. Use a protective canvas case or roll to store equipment such as pencils, a dip pen, and sable brushes safely. Take a hard surface, such as a wooden drawing board, and clips to secure the paper and support your hand as you draw.

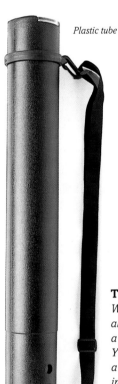

*Plastic tube*

*Canvas roll*

*Collapsible wooden stool*

### Transporting paper
*When carrying paper, always protect it by using a folder or a plastic tube. You should also include a can or bottle of fixative in your kit to prevent finished drawings from smudging while they are stored together.*

### Canvas roll
*A protective roll is the easiest way of transporting your drawing materials. The rolls are usually made from canvas with elastic strips sewn in to hold individual items securely. You may also want to take a small wooden stool if you are going to be working outdoors for any length of time.*

*Drawing board*

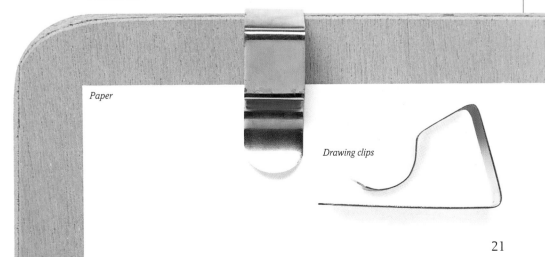

*Paper*

*Drawing clips*

### Drawing board
*Although it may be the bulkiest piece of equipment, a drawing board is one of the most important items to include in your kit and is a cheaper and more convenient alternative than a wooden or metal easel. Another option is to use a block of watercolor paper, which is sold with each sheet of paper lightly glued to the next to give a solid, flat surface on which to draw.*

# Gallery of Drawing Media

Often the subject matter you draw will dictate what type of medium you use. A piece of detailed architecture can be drawn most precisely with a technical pen or a fine nib, and charcoal proves itself a superior medium for swiftly capturing the mood of a person. For an elegant, rhythmical drawing of a moving figure, brush and ink offers the widest range of expressive line. Occasionally mixing your media can introduce a whole new facet to your work, but the success of mixing different media together depends upon using each to its best advantage. A pencil sketch can evolve into a more substantial drawing if you add watercolor to strengthen the image, or add colored pencils or chalks to build up the texture in a series of hatched lines. Startling effects can be created by using a heavily textured paper with pastels and crayons in an array of vivid colors.

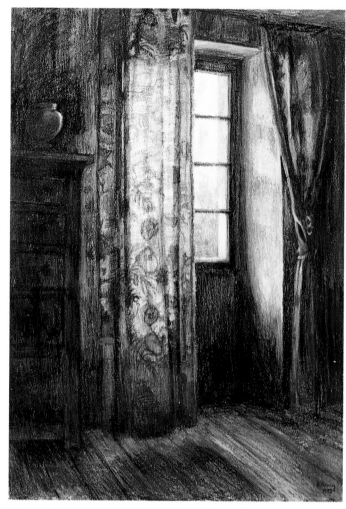

**Karen Raney, *Les Planes Bedroom Window*** *34 x 24 in (86 x 61 cm)*
*The careful way in which these oil pastels have been applied in layers has resulted in a brilliance of color and a strong tonal pattern that enlivens the work.*

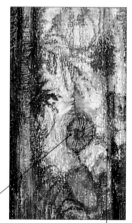

**A sgraffito** technique has been used to scrape away some of the oil pastel color and produce bright highlights.

**The oil pastels** pick up the tooth of this textured paper so that tiny areas of white paper cause the colors to shimmer with light.

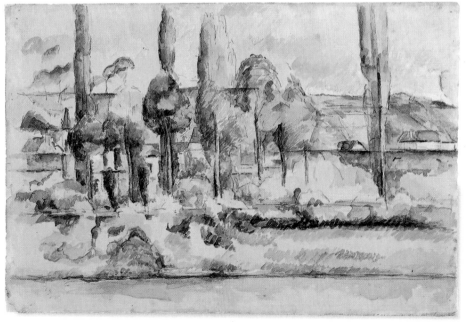

**Paul Cézanne, *The Castle of Médan*, 1879/80** *12 x 18½ in (31 x 47 cm)*
*Although the majority of Cézanne's watercolor drawings are quite slight, they are full of structure and power. In this study, pencil marks have been reinforced with watercolor to give a strong image that combines a lightness of feeling and a wide sense of space.*

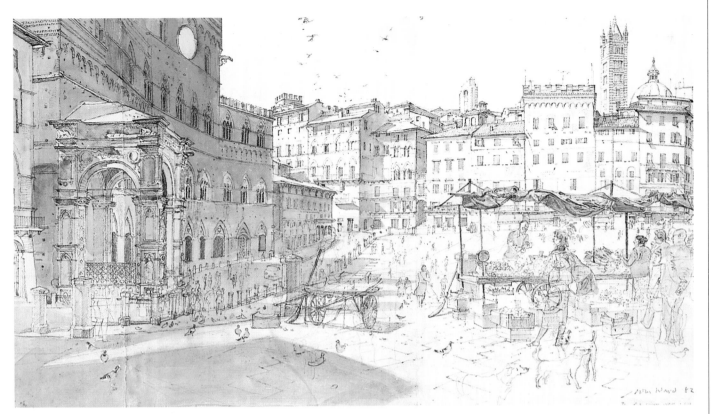

**John Ward, RA,** *Siena* *13 x 22 in (33 x 56 cm)*
*In this picture, the artist has caught the dazzlingly bright
light that shines on a bustling market square with a
clever combination of watercolor and pencil. Rich,
deep washes of watercolor have been drawn in shaded
areas to heighten the contrast with the stark white paper,
while clean pencil marks delineate the structure of
the ornate Italian buildings precisely.*

**Jane Stanton,** *Horace Shadow Boxing*

*11 x 9 in (28 x 23cm)*
*This vigorous drawing in black and white chalks has been
built up in a series of rhythmical marks. Interestingly, the
white of the paper has been left untouched to depict the
bandaged hands, while the highlights on the arm and
shoulder have been produced by white chalk. This gives the
figure a sense of solidity and heightens the tonal contrasts.*

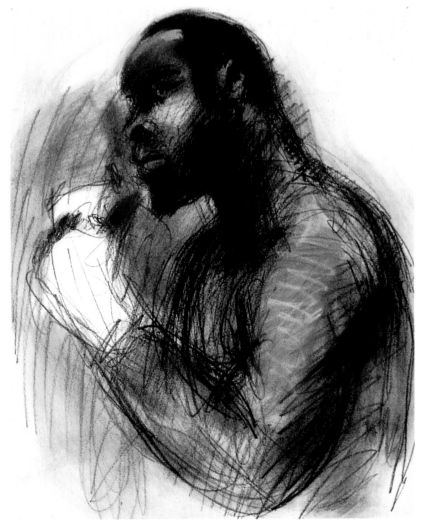

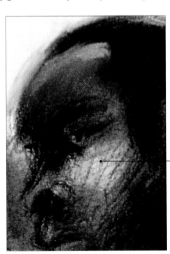

**The contrast**
of intense black
shading and lightly
drawn linear marks
creates a strong
sense of movement.

23

# PAPER

ORIGINALLY ALL PAPERS were handmade and tended to be of high quality. Paper was also quite scarce, so artists often drew on the reverse side for economy. Toned or colored paper, prepared by the artist himself with washes of watercolor, was a popular way of creating unusual effects. Today we have an enormous range of papers to choose from, which can make the choice a difficult one. Both handmade and commercially made papers have varying degrees of absorbency and are sold in different weights. Toned or tinted papers are also worth considering, and they are available in a selection of colors. Experiment with textures and weights until you find paper suitable for your technique.

## Toned paper
*Toned or colored paper can add an extra dimension to a work, providing a uniform tone and an underlying unity as well as influencing the mood of a drawing. Special artists' papers, such as Ingres paper, are best for this type of drawing.*

*Commercially made smooth paper*

*Selection of colored pastel papers and toned watercolor papers*

*Commercially made semi-rough paper*

*Cartridge paper*

*Handmade semi-rough paper*

## Texture
*There are three types of commercially made paper: smooth or hot-pressed (HP); semi-rough or cold-pressed (NOT); and rough. Choose a texture that suits the medium you use; strokes of watercolor emphasize the grain of roughly textured handmade paper, while pen and ink requires a smoother surface to ensure that the ink flows smoothly. Try to buy acid-free paper so that it will not darken with age.*

*Commercially made textured paper*

*Roughly textured handmade paper*

## Making a sketchbook

Sketchbooks can be quite expensive to buy and may contain the wrong kind of paper for your drawing needs. By making your own sketchbooks, you can choose the size, weight, and absorbency of paper that best suits your style and media. Use wallpaper samples or wrapping paper to cover the outside of the book.

1 ◀ Cut out two identical pieces of cardboard for the front and back covers, and one long strip for the spine. Then cut and fold the drawing paper and check to see that it fits within the covers before binding it together.

### Materials

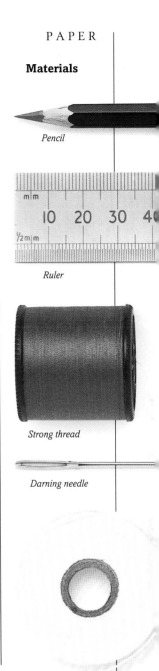

*Pencil*

*Ruler*

*Strong thread*

*Darning needle*

*Fabric tape*
*Wallpaper*
*Strong material*

*Stiff cardboard*
*Textured paper*

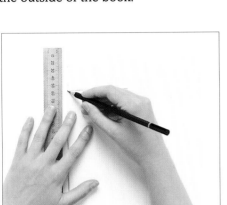

2 ◀ Measure the width of the binding tape first. Then place a ruler by the folded edges of the paper and divide the length into five. Mark the tape width at each section with a pencil.

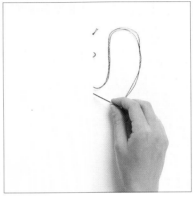

3 ▶ Bind the pages with a needle and thread, leaving small loops along the edge of the folds.

4 ▶ Slip small pieces of tape through each loop and then tighten and secure the thread. You can use any type of fabric tape so long as it is strong and adheres securely to the cardboard covers.

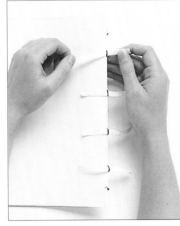

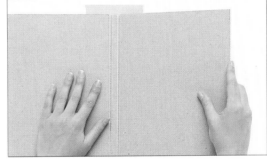

5 ▲ Glue the pieces of cardboard onto a long section of strong fabric, leaving a slight gap on both sides of the cardboard strip to create a join.

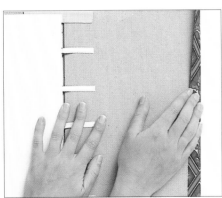

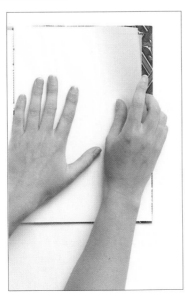

6 ▲ Secure each piece of tape to either side of the cardboard and glue the overlaps of the wallpaper down.

7 ▶ Neaten the inside covers by gluing a clean sheet of paper over the seams and tape.

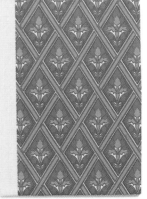

### Specialized sketchbooks
*Try making a variety of sketchbooks in different sizes with a selection of textured or colored papers.*

# GALLERY OF PAPER

THE TEXTURE OF PAPER can easily affect the look of a drawing, and it is worth thinking about which type of paper to use for each particular medium. Using a smooth paper for pen work prevents the tip of the nib from scratching through the surface, while textured paper readily breaks up any lines or marks and suits media such as chalk and pastel. The absorbency and weight of a paper is important to note before using it with watercolor, as it determines the best way to handle the paint and how long a drawing should be worked on. Toned paper can also influence the look and mood of a drawing, serving either to heighten opaque highlights or to exist as a halftone.

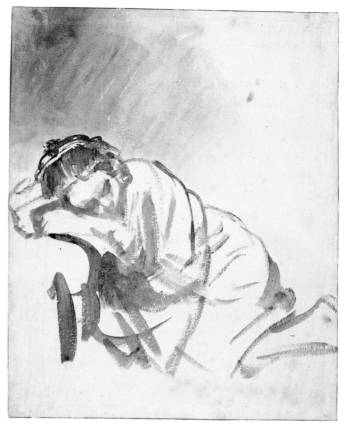

**Rembrandt, *A Girl Sleeping*, c.1655-6** *10 x 9 in (25 x 20 cm)*
*Rembrandt's brush drawings have an almost unbelievably assured and spontaneous quality about them. This drawing in brown wash demonstrates how well the artist utilized his materials, producing a sensuous drawing of simple lines brought alive by the textured paper. The high absorbency of the paper meant that Rembrandt had to draw swiftly and confidently as the watercolor soaked into the surface; the paper's rough, grainy texture is emphasized by the dragged quality of each line as the paint catches on the tooth.*

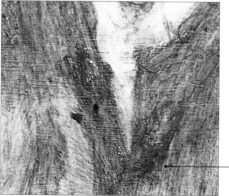

**The resilient quality** that gesso primer gives this paper has enabled the artist to rework details and scratch out areas to increase the rough texture of the drawing.

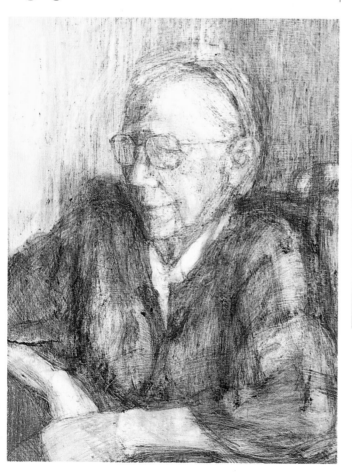

**Karen Raney, *Mrs. Robb*** *14 x 11 in (36 x 28 cm)*
*This drawing relies heavily upon a particular technical approach, with the paper primed first with acrylic gesso to give a controlled, significant texture. This resistant surface allows the artist to explore her subject in a vigorous style, reworking the figure as needed with oil pastels in a series of lines and hatchings that are accentuated by the textured paper.*

**Kay Gallwey,** *Spanish Dancer* 20 x 30 in (51 x 76 cm)
*This work is a fine example of how the quality and color of paper can influence a drawing; the pale gray tone of this surface heightens the opaque areas of white gouache while still allowing the more transparent strokes of watercolor to show up. Although it is as absorbent as the paper Rembrandt used, the smoother consistency of this paper allows the artist to draw lyrically, producing lengthy, more generous brushstrokes. The highlights on the cheek and hair are also highly effective against the subtle gray color of the paper.*

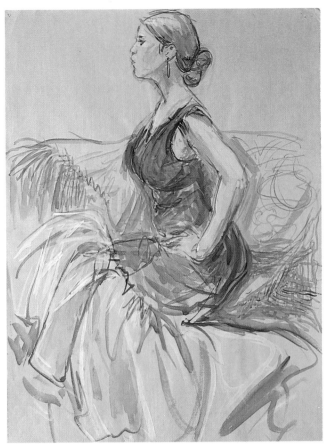

**The smooth, absorbent** quality of the paper brings out the stylish strokes of watercolor.

**Here the artist** has utilized the colored paper as a halftone on the hand by building up tones of watercolor around an area of untouched paper.

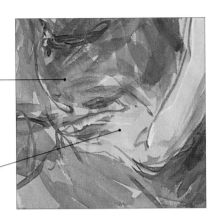

**Percy Horton,** *Study of a Farmyard,* **1935** 12 x 18 in (30 x 46 cm)
*Drawn on fine Ingres paper, this study in graphite pencil and gray wash reveals the smoothness of the surface. The artist has used the gentle texture of the paper to help build up this drawing in an intricate style, incorporating finer details and precise information to produce a strong and interesting composition.*

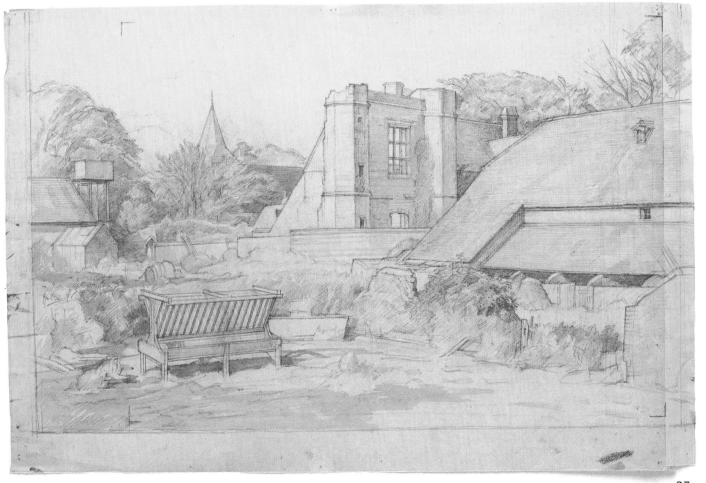

# WAYS OF WORKING

Drawing is a skill that improves with practice, and the more knowledge you have about your materials, the better your drawing will be. For example, your choice of pencil, pen and ink, or Conté crayon will affect the look of your drawing, and it may be that one medium suits your purpose better than another. You will need to work with the different materials to familiarize yourself with them, to discover what each is capable of, and to see which you feel most comfortable with. Pen and ink is ideal for fine, delicate lines, whereas a brush and ink can range from fine lines to broad sweeps of tone. Once you know the strengths and limitations of your materials, you can choose the appropriate medium for your subject matter and for the mood you wish to create. You will then be able to start a piece of work with a positive idea about how the subject relates to the medium.

### Materials to suit your style

Of course each individual will view life differently, and two artists faced with the same subject would probably choose different media depending on how they perceive what they see and how they wish to portray it. Rembrandt, for example, used a loaded brush of ink to make rapid notations of fleeting effects and images. You can try to do the same, or make loose strokes with watercolor washes. Like ink, these will produce an effect very quickly, which can then be drawn over with a pencil or pen. You may be more methodical and analytical in your approach, and prefer the control that you can keep with a pencil. Many artists like to map out their drawings with great precision, and for this a pencil, a ruler, and an eraser are the perfect tools.

### Choosing the right paper

Do not underestimate the importance of your paper. If you work on smooth paper your pencil will be able to flow uninterrupted over its surface. You will be able to modulate your lines without any unexpected effects. A disadvantage to smooth paper, however, is that large areas of tone may seem somewhat flat. A textured paper is just the reverse: used in conjunction with charcoal or chalks, it gives a lively, broken characteristic to lines or areas of tone. Take note of the weight of the paper too, so that if you use watercolors, for example, the paper will be heavy enough not to buckle.

## Drawing with watercolor

The point at which a drawing ceases to be a drawing and becomes a painting is both a philosophical issue and a practical one. You can "draw" with color using colored pencils, pastels, or chalks, or you can add color to what are essentially linear drawings. You can essentially mix and match – start with pencil and add a watercolor wash, or start with watercolors and strengthen certain details later with pen and ink. By combining such media in this way, you can build up a more substantial drawing and create dramatic effects.

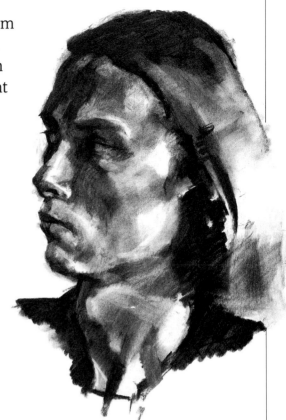

### Procedures

Just as there are endless possibilities when mixing media, so too are there quite different procedures. There are no rules about what you can and cannot use, and no set order to how you work with your materials. For instance, you could start a drawing with a pencil, then perhaps add some watercolor. You could then refine the drawing with pen and ink and perhaps crosshatch over certain areas with chalks or pastels to create different textures.

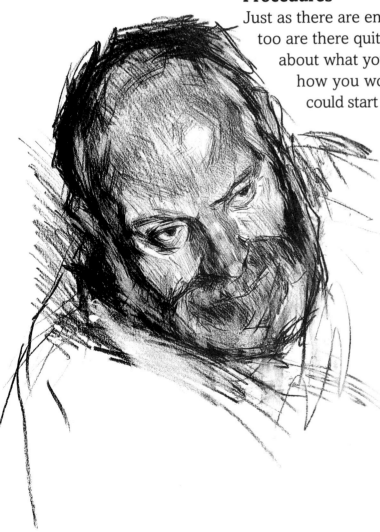

### Mixing media

Working in this way, you introduce a new medium at various intervals because it strengthens the previous one or creates a new, interesting look. On the other hand, you could make a decision from the outset to combine a selection of materials and use them in conjunction with each other. It is a question of what effect you wish to achieve and the best way to go about it. As with your drawing skills, learning to make the most of your materials is a matter of time, practice, and pleasure.

29

# GETTING STARTED

LEARNING TO DRAW IS ULTIMATELY about learning how to see and interpret the world around you; it is vital that you observe images correctly if you want to be able to draw convincingly. Train your eye to look for specific factors as you analyze objects or a scene. You need to be able to distill the information and translate it into an original drawing, in your own distinctive style and from your own personal perspective. The best way to begin practicing this process is to take a sketchbook everywhere you go, and jot down ideas and sketches for future drawings. Use drawing materials that you are familiar with so that you can concentrate more on how you perceive an image and start to gain confidence in your drawing.

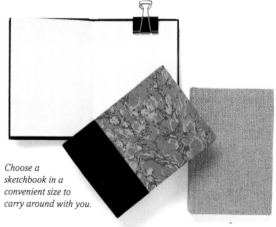

*Choose a sketchbook in a convenient size to carry around with you.*

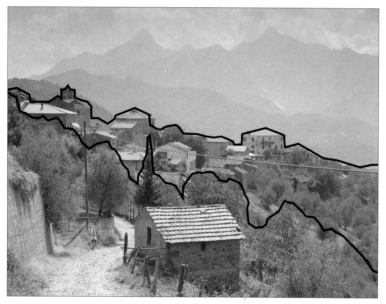

### Looking for depth
*Every scene consists of a foreground, a middle ground, and a background (shown by the black outlines, left). Features in the foreground are large and clearly visible, objects in the middle ground appear smaller and less conspicuous, and images in the distance are hazy and undefined. In drawing on a two-dimensional surface, these three divisions create the necessary illusion of depth. Another way to detect these divisions is to look for an intensity of color: the foreground often consists of strong, powerful hues, while the background is full of pale, often bluish tones. This atmospheric condition is known as aerial perspective.*

### The changing effects of light
*The effect of light on an object or a scene is crucial: it can throw whole areas into obscurity, or illuminate one aspect so that it appears to radiate and shimmer. It is worth observing how the sun moves across an object through the course of one day, noting how radically its appearance alters. A variety of warm and cool colors and elongated shapes and shadows transform the look of this building (right) according to the particular time of day. This exercise should help you judge the best moment to draw a scene or create a particular mood.*

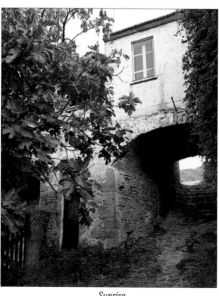

*Sunrise*

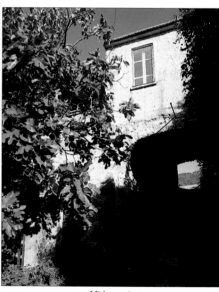

*Mid-morning*

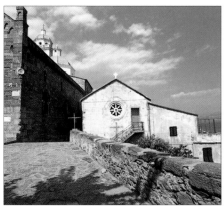

**High viewpoint**
*The viewpoint you choose significantly affects the look of a drawing. A high viewpoint allows you to look down on a scene, which can often create a sense of space and harmony.*

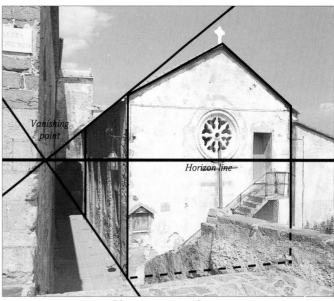

Vanishing point

Horizon line

**Linear perspective**
*Linear perspective is a theory based on how we perceive an object or a scene from a particular viewpoint. The building above recedes in space and seems to grow smaller, yet in reality the sides of the building are parallel. If lines are drawn along these sides, they converge at a distant point known as a vanishing point. A horizontal line across the vanishing point indicates the eye level from which the object is viewed. This theory enables you to represent a three-dimensional image on a flat surface.*

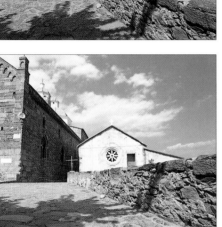

**Normal viewpoint**
*A normal viewpoint – the eye level of an individual standing upright – creates a familiar sense of human perspective. Distant features may be obscured by areas of foreground.*

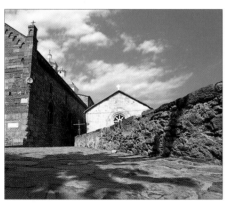

**Low viewpoint**
*If you draw from a low viewpoint, the objects around you will appear bolder and more imposing, creating a strong psychological impact.*

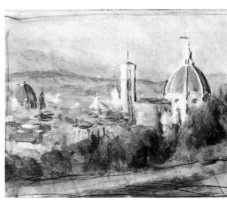

**Using a sketchbook**
*This watercolor sketch of Florence, Italy, features a high viewpoint, linear and aerial perspective, and describes the changing effects of light across the city.*

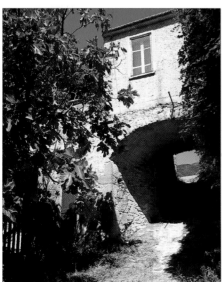

*Midday*

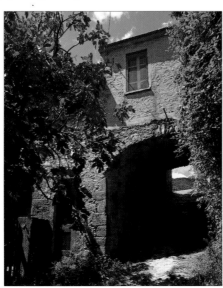

*Afternoon*

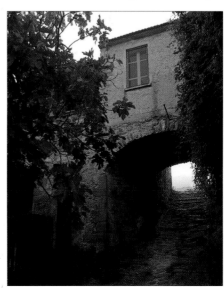

*Early evening*

# THE BASICS OF DRAWING

MUCH OF WHAT WE SEE around us can be simplified on paper into a series of very basic shapes. The most obvious shapes are cubes and spheres, and it is helpful to see objects in these terms when you begin to draw. Regular box shapes with parallel sides are quite easy to practice drawing, and a basic understanding of linear perspective and converging lines will enable you to create a better sense of structure and depth. Rounded objects are more complex as they should be constructed from a series of ellipses which can be quite hard to draw correctly at first. However, the best way to become comfortable with drawing solid objects is to gather a collection of household items and practice drawing their different shapes.

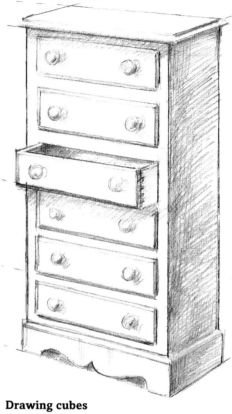

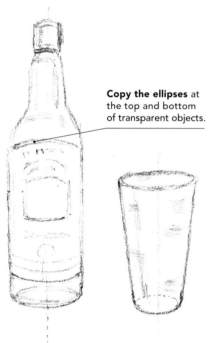

**Copy the ellipses** at the top and bottom of transparent objects.

### Drawing ellipses

It is worth spending some time practicing ellipses so that you can gain confidence drawing round objects. Ellipses are in fact foreshortened circles and change their nature according to your eye level (*see below*). The principle of foreshortening is that the width of an ellipse remains the same, but its apparent height reduces the farther it tilts away from you. The easiest way to draw an ellipse is to sketch it roughly and then slice it in half, first vertically, then horizontally. You can then refine it until each quarter is the mirror image of its neighbor. Make sure each corner remains rounded

### Drawing cubes

*This chest of drawers is composed of straight, parallel sides that appear to grow smaller as they recede into space. Converging lines drawn as guides can help you get the right perspective.*

and that the middle section doesn't look too flattened. Practice drawing an empty bottle or a glass so you can actually see the foreshortened ellipses through the transparent material.

### Changing ellipses

*Look at a glass from directly above, then below. The nature of its ellipses will change considerably. If you lean over the glass and view it at an angle, the ellipses will be quite rounded and circular; viewed from the side, they are at an extreme and are very foreshortened. Ellipses at the rim and the base of an object are never quite identical: the nearer an ellipse is to your eye level, the thinner it is; the farther away, the more circular it is. View the glass from below to see this effect.*

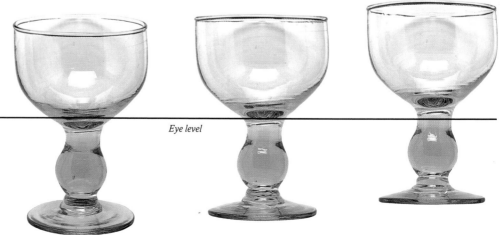

Eye level

## Intersecting ellipses

To re-create the roundness of an object you need to imagine two ellipses, one horizontal, one vertical. The teapot, for example, is made up of a flattened circle for its basic form and then intersected at right angles by a second ellipse. The problem with drawing an object such as this teapot is its opaque nature, so you have to imagine the progression of the second ellipse through the back of the object and judge how foreshortened it actually is. This skill becomes easier with practice. Check your eye level and, if necessary, draw a faint guideline across the sketch to signify the angle from which you draw so that you create the right shapes.

**Multiple ellipses**
*A complicated object such as this cocktail shaker, with sides curving in and out, should be constructed of several foreshortened ellipses at different angles and in varying sizes.*

**Obscured ellipses**
*Each ellipse has been fully drawn in this sketch of two opaque objects – even though in reality the back of the plate is obscured by the bowl. Once the subject has been drawn accurately, this line can be erased.*

**Guidelines**
*Use faint guidelines to establish the center of the drawing and the angle at which additional features should align.*

## Still life

*Arrange an interesting collection of objects when you feel confident enough to draw several items together. If you want to draw imaginary ellipses through opaque objects, you may need to erase them when you have finished drawing, to give each object a better sense of solidity.*

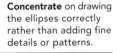

**Concentrate** on drawing the ellipses correctly rather than adding fine details or patterns.

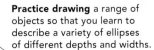

**Practice drawing** a range of objects so that you learn to describe a variety of ellipses of different depths and widths.

# LINEAR DRAWING

A LINE IS THE MOST basic form of representation in drawing, yet the power and versatility possible with the drawn line means that it has a wide range of descriptive possibilities. Linear drawing is essentially a technique that uses line, rather than the depth of color, as the main vehicle of expression. Lines can be drawn with great spontaneity, or they can be eloquent, economical, or even decorative. Shadows and highlights can also be suggested with a series of heavy or sensitive lines. A good line drawing will convey explicitly what the artist wants to express or describe.

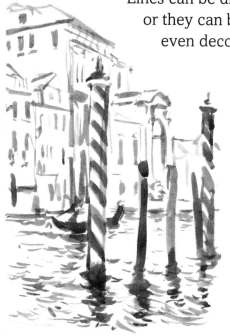

**Brush drawing**
*This canal scene is deftly developed with simple brushmarks. Notice the variation in strength and tone between the bold strokes on the poles and the gentle ripples of water.*

### The descriptive power of line
The drawn line can be very adaptable, providing the artist with a vast vocabulary when drawing. Strong, straight lines can be bold and dramatic; sensitive lines may evoke moods and atmosphere or convey lyrical qualities; and curved fluid lines can describe elegant contours. Once you have decided what you want to draw, choose the most suitable materials to either

**Charcoal study**
*The soft, fluid lines of this charcoal drawing suitably capture the expression and the suppleness of this young child. Lines on the child's hair and dress are economically applied to suggest texture while other areas are weighted with thick line to give a sense of depth.*

emphasize the illusion of solidity and weight or clarify delicate details and touches through lightly drawn lines. Experiment with different media until you find one that suits your style.

**Technical pen sketch**
*You can create clear, well-defined lines with a technical pen. Here the figures are loosely sketched to capture the spontaneity of the scene. There is a roughness to the lines that evokes a sense of immediacy.*

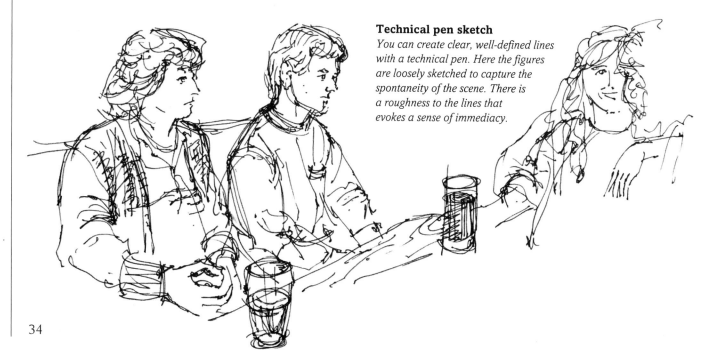

## Drawing with pen and ink

Ink applied with a pen is a popular drawing medium. The ink comes in a range of colors, just as steel nibs come in a variety of thicknesses. It is best to use cartridge paper so that the nib does not become stuck in the fibers.

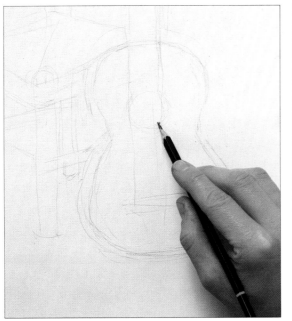

1 ▶ If you are unsure of drawing directly in pen and ink, start off with a light pencil sketch. This will allow you to make sure your proportions are correct and that you are happy with the composition. It will also train you to be observant.

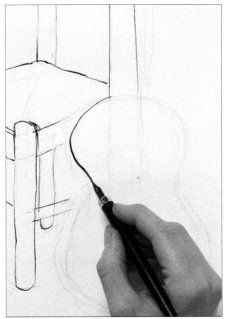

2 ▲ Define the shape of the chair with clean straight lines, and in contrast, draw the contours of the guitar with gently curved lines. You may have to apply more pressure to the nib when drawing curved lines to allow the ink to flow easily.

### Guitar and Chair

*This simple composition lends itself to an interesting interplay of straight and curved lines. The rigid form of the chair, drawn with vertical and horizontal lines, serves to accentuate the curvaceous outlines of the guitar. The overall effect is a pleasing balance of strong form and pure line.*

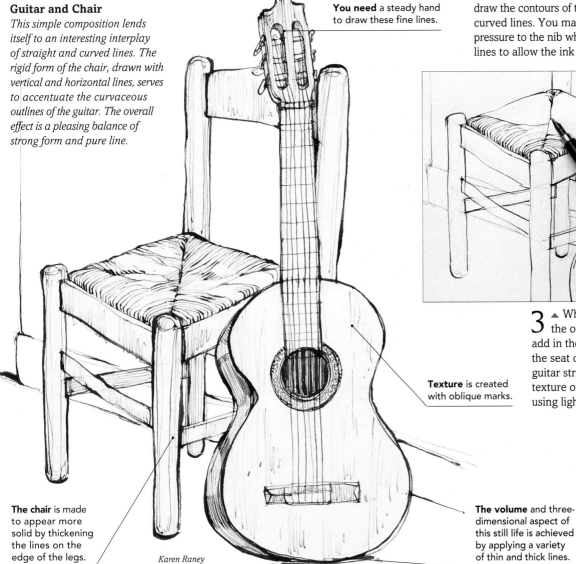

**You need** a steady hand to draw these fine lines.

3 ▲ When you have drawn the outlines of both objects, add in the finer details, such as the seat of the chair and the guitar strings. Suggest the texture of the rush matting by using light and dark strokes.

**Texture** is created with oblique marks.

**The chair** is made to appear more solid by thickening the lines on the edge of the legs.

*Karen Raney*

**The volume** and three-dimensional aspect of this still life is achieved by applying a variety of thin and thick lines.

### Materials

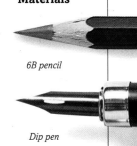

*6B pencil*

*Dip pen*

# FORM & MODELING

FORM IS A TERM that is used to describe the visual appearance and shape of something. In a drawing, form can be represented with lines and as a series of tones (a range of values from light to dark) known as modeling. Modeling indicates the solidity and three-dimensional quality of a form, which is often enhanced or accentuated by light hitting the form and creating shadows. There are several different techniques to use for modeling, depending on which type of media you choose. Each medium gives a characteristic set of marks, but materials that cover the paper easily, such as pastels and watercolor, are good for large areas of shading, while colored pencils, which cannot be blended, are best used for feathering or crosshatching.

**Solid shading**
*This sketch of a woman's back has been modeled into a three-dimensional form by lightly shading solid areas of tone with a pencil. The weighted contour lines also emphasize the volume of the figure. A less linear way of applying tone, this type of shading can be sensitive and subtle.*

### Describing form
Although the appearance and solidity of a subject can be suggested by drawing purely with line, a more substantial representation of its form can be achieved with modeling. Look for different textures and any deep tones before you start to draw so that you choose materials and techniques which best depict the smooth curves of a woman's back, for example, or a crumpled piece of material.

*Solid shading*

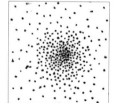
*Stippling*

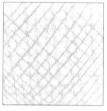
*Crosshatching*

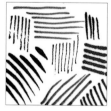
*Hatching*

### Mark-making
*There are several ways to shade an image to create a sense of solidity. Hatching, crosshatching, and feathering are variations of a series of parallel lines drawn close to one another. Stippling is a technique whereby dots rather than lines form an image. Sgraffito, meaning scratched, can be similar to hatching.*

**Crosshatching**
*Crosshatching is a form of hatching, combining two or more sets of parallel lines that cross one another at an angle. They can be used to create a sense of form or, when using two or more colors, to produce secondary colors as the strokes intersect and mix optically.*

**The crosshatching** on this leg gives it a much stronger sense of form and solidity than the outline of the other leg.

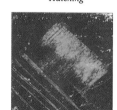
*Sgraffito*

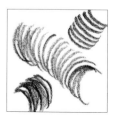
*Bracelet shading*

*Feathering*

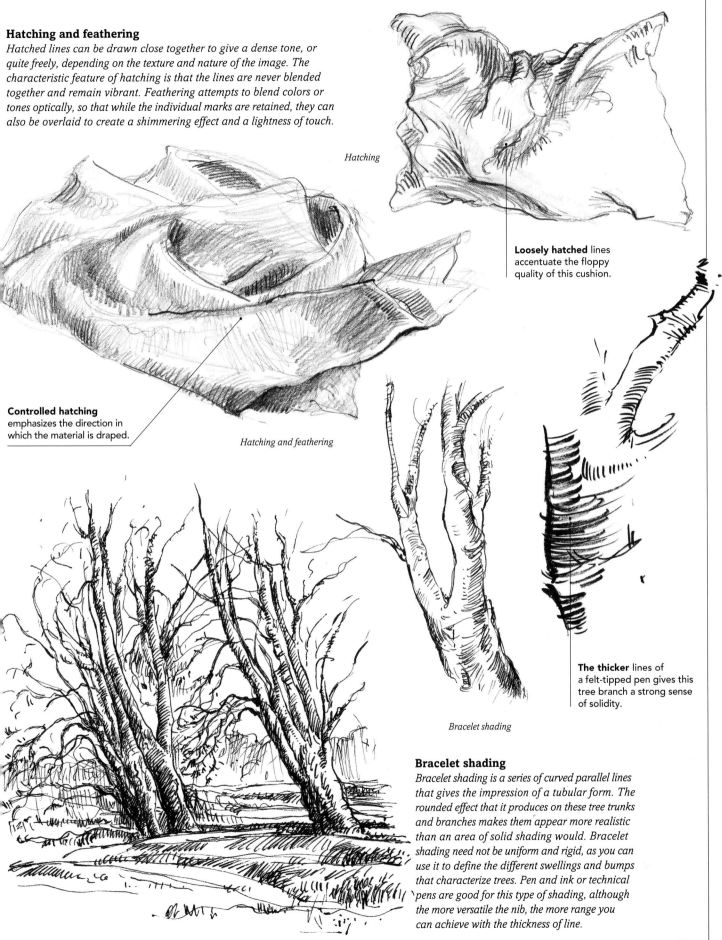

## Hatching and feathering

*Hatched lines can be drawn close together to give a dense tone, or quite freely, depending on the texture and nature of the image. The characteristic feature of hatching is that the lines are never blended together and remain vibrant. Feathering attempts to blend colors or tones optically, so that while the individual marks are retained, they can also be overlaid to create a shimmering effect and a lightness of touch.*

*Hatching*

**Loosely hatched** lines accentuate the floppy quality of this cushion.

**Controlled hatching** emphasizes the direction in which the material is draped.

*Hatching and feathering*

**The thicker** lines of a felt-tipped pen gives this tree branch a strong sense of solidity.

*Bracelet shading*

## Bracelet shading

*Bracelet shading is a series of curved parallel lines that gives the impression of a tubular form. The rounded effect that it produces on these tree trunks and branches makes them appear more realistic than an area of solid shading would. Bracelet shading need not be uniform and rigid, as you can use it to define the different swellings and bumps that characterize trees. Pen and ink or technical pens are good for this type of shading, although the more versatile the nib, the more range you can achieve with the thickness of line.*

37

# TONAL DRAWING

To UNDERSTAND THE VARYING degrees of darkness and light known as tonal values, it is essential to observe the effects of light and shadows falling on the objects you draw. You can then construct a drawing using areas of tone to describe shapes and to model forms so that they appear three-dimensional. Tonal drawings often tend to be more about mood and atmosphere, where whole areas can be suffused with light or submerged in deep shadows. A drawing may also be enhanced by using specific areas of contrast to create a tonal pattern throughout the composition. The important thing to remember about tonal drawing is to draw the minimum of lines and keep the emphasis on shapes and forms. Use tones as a painter would use colors to project images and to express a mood.

### Lighting effects

To create the appropriate effects of strong light on a still life composition, it is important to set up the lighting at an angle that will maximize the presence of highlights and deep shadows. It is this contrast that will allow you the potential to explore tonal patterns in your arrangement. Use a soft dark pencil for shading the darkest forms and a kneaded eraser to create highlights by lifting out some of the tonal marks to reveal the brilliance of the white paper. The subtle shading of dark and light tones gives solidity to forms and atmosphere to your drawing.

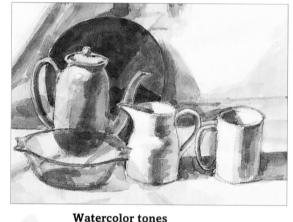

### Watercolor tones

*This monochromatic watercolor sketch of the same still life illustrates how a similar effect of light and shade can be achieved by using just three tones. Limiting yourself to such a small selection of tones will help you look closely for strong shapes and effective tonal contrasts.*

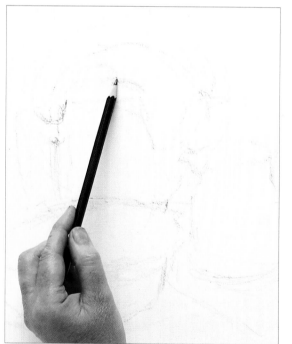

1 ▲ Begin by studying the shapes of the objects and also observe the play of light across their surfaces. With a soft pencil, make a series of loose marks to establish the scale of the arrangement of objects in relation to the size of the paper. Start with the largest object, the plate, so you can use it as a gauge to draw the other objects to scale.

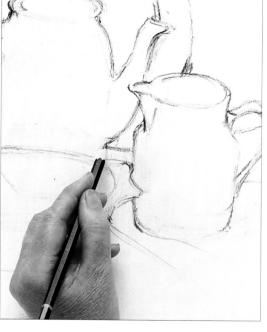

2 ◀ Redefine the loose sketch with stronger lines once you are happy with the composition. At this stage use a lighter pencil to accentuate the contours, such as the spout of the coffee-pot. These outlines serve as a framework for modeling the objects by shading with light and dark tones.

3 ▶ Add a light gray tone by using gentle sweeping strokes with the side of the pencil. Once this is established you can deepen the tone for shadows and erase it for highlights. Explore the shapes that the shadows make between the objects: darkening the shadows will push the objects forward and make them look less flat. Develop the gradated tones on the objects, from the lightest to the darkest, to give them volume.

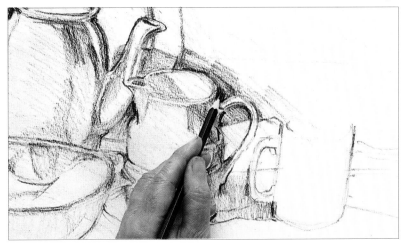

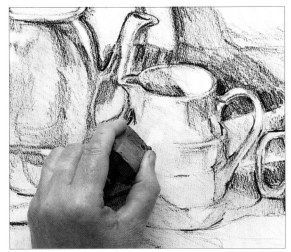

4 ▲ Now bring out the soft highlights on the pitcher by lifting out some of the tonal marks with the tip of a kneaded eraser. This is an effective way of "drawing" the light areas, using the white of the paper as the lightest tint in the tonal scale. These highlights will illuminate every object, as well as imbuing the drawing with a strong sense of light.

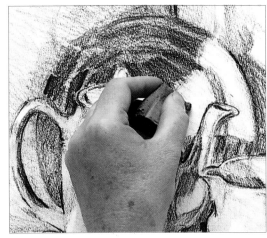

5 ◀ At this last stage refine the shadow edges on the plate with the kneaded eraser so that the darkest tones blend in subtly with the mid- and light tones to create a pleasing tonal effect. The shadows also enhance the sense of solidity of the plate.

## Tonal Study

*The three-dimensional quality of this still life drawing is achieved mainly by shading rather than by drawing with lines. The texture and form of each of the objects are developed and molded by employing a subtle range of tonal contrasts. An illusion of space and depth is also created by the careful positioning of shadows.*

**Main materials**

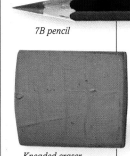

*7B pencil*

*Kneaded eraser*

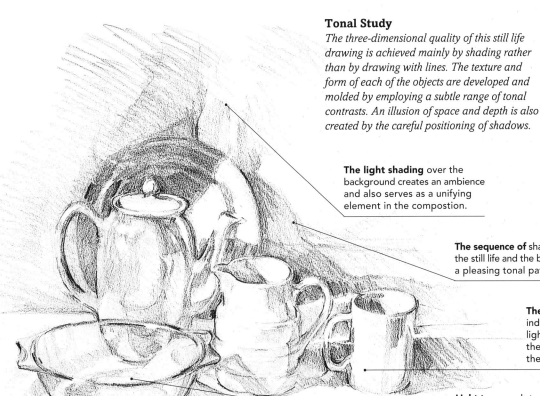

**The light shading** over the background creates an ambience and also serves as a unifying element in the compostion.

**The sequence of** shadows cast across the still life and the background forms a pleasing tonal pattern.

**The highlights not** only indicate the direction of light but also describe the smooth sheen of the ceramic objects.

**Light tones** and strong highlights capture the transparency of the glass dish and give the impression of reflected light.

*Sue Sareen*

# GALLERY OF FORM

STRICTLY SPEAKING, the term *form* refers to the visual aspect and shape of an image, but within the realm of drawing it can also incorporate a sculptural quality: during the Renaissance and Baroque periods, the emphasis in art was on creating as solid and three-dimensional an image as possible. Michelangelo's work has a powerful feeling of shape and structure that goes well beyond a superficial rendering of the human body. This idea of sculpted form is still relevant to drawing today, although it is often interpreted differently. The quality of line may be more expressive and economical and may suggest movement more dramatically.

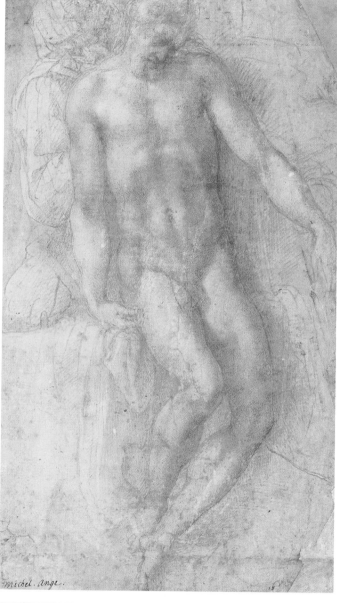

**Michelangelo,**
***Drawing for a Late Pietà, c.1530s*** *15¾ x 9 in (40 x 23 cm)*
*One of the greatest artists of the Renaissance, Michelangelo concentrated on the human figure almost exclusively and his anatomical knowledge was impressive. This perfectly proportioned image of Christ is caught by a diffused light that highlights the complexity of muscle and bone structure forming his body. The artist has modeled these features into a dynamic image that still exudes power in spite of the lifeless state of the figure.*

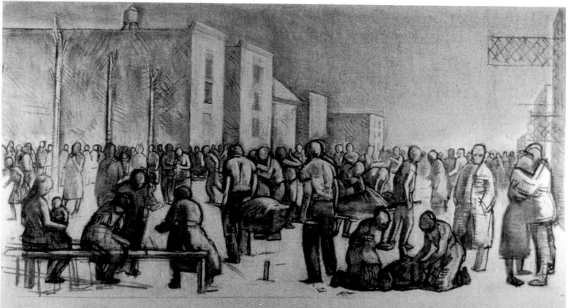

**Thomas Newbolt,**
***Study for "Bomb"***
*16 x 28 in (41 x 71 cm)*
*Even at first glance, this drawing has a wonderful sense of structure and strength. The artist has drawn the figures simply, with thick, heavy outlines so that they seem to create form collectively. He has kept details to a minimum, imbuing the scene with drama despite the anonymity of the figures.*

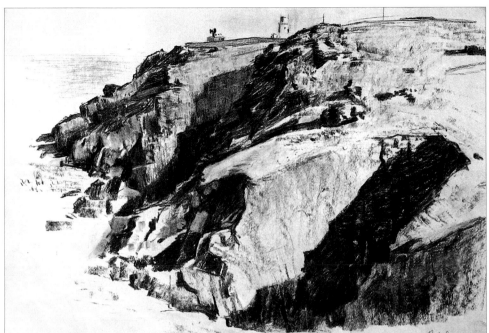

**Paul Lewin, *Penwith Coast,***
*17 x 20 in (43 x 51 cm)*
*Rock formations, with their stark, craggy shapes and dramatic shadows, are a wonderful subject for studying form. The depth and drama of this drawing relies upon a bright light that picks out the eroding coastline as a series of unusual and abstract images. Deep shadows help build up a strong tonal pattern that combines with the highlights to give a three-dimensional form with a striking presence.*

**Donald Hamilton Fraser RA,**
***Dancer Rehearsing Juliet*** *18 x 20 in (46 x 51 cm)*
*Watching dancers or acrobats is a good way to study the human form as it moves. Here the artist has made a sensitive yet elegant study of a dancer caught midway through a sequence. The essence of the power in this drawing is in the economy of line that describes the form of the body succinctly. Areas such as the hands and legs assume a sense of solidity despite the simplicity of line.*

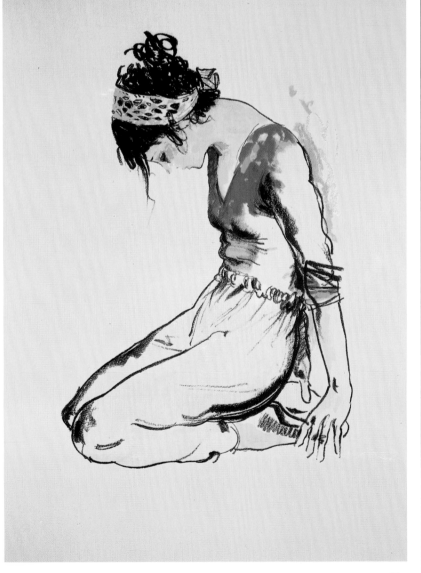

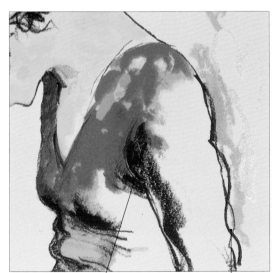

**Thick, simple lines** of chalk across the upper body suggest shadows and create a realistic sense of shape and depth.

**A repeated line** along the arm echoes the constant movement of the dancer.

41

# LAYOUT & CONSTRUCTION

THE LAYOUT, OR COMPOSITION, of a drawing should provide a balanced order of shapes, colors, and forms. Use a viewfinder to choose the most appropriate scene and then draw the layout by measuring every feature carefully.

Measuring is an essential element in the construction of a drawing: it provides a scale by which to judge the relationship and proportions of different masses. Objects can be visually measured with the end of a pencil.

IT IS OFTEN DIFFICULT to select just a few elements of a landscape for a drawing, so use a viewfinder to crop the scene in front of you.

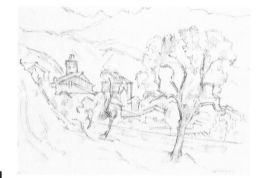

**Using a viewfinder**
*A viewfinder made from cardboard (left) helps you select the part of a scene you wish to draw, and it can be adjusted to different proportions. The amount you see through the frame varies according to how close you hold it to your eye and how you adjust the two L shapes. Make a quick pencil sketch of this cropped image if you want to make sure the composition works well.*

*Adjust the two L-shapes of the viewfinder until you have selected the most suitable composition.*

**Measuring**
*If you work on a large composition, or from sketches and photographs, you may prefer to establish a scale to measure the different components of a scene. However, if you draw directly from life, try using a "sight size" technique. This involves measuring the size of an image exactly as you see it with the end of a pencil or a ruler. Transfer the measurement onto paper so that the image is an identical size.*

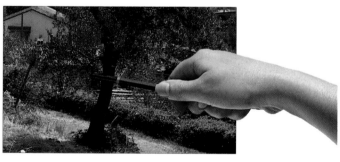

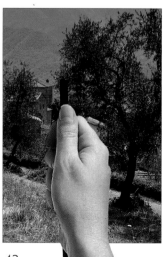

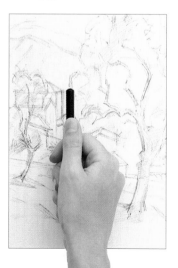

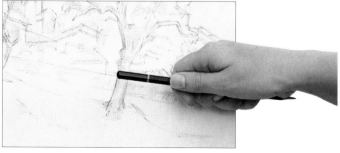

## Drawing a series of buildings from life

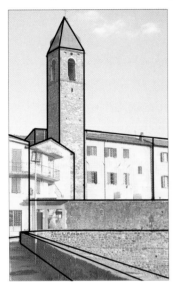

Drawing from life can be both stimulating and problematic, so plan your composition carefully and measure constantly until your eye becomes practiced at judging size and scale.

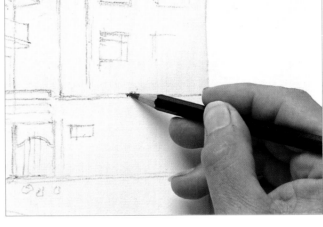

**1** ▶ Draw the outlines of these buildings as a series of simple lines on a large piece of semi-rough paper with a soft pencil.

### Deconstructing an image

*A scene such as this group of buildings may at first appear quite complex and rather daunting, but if you can reduce it to a series of simple shapes and three-dimensional blocks in your mind, you will gain a better sense of perspective and structure as you begin to draw.*

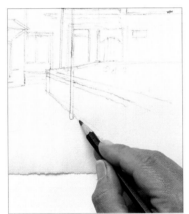

**2** ◀ The wall in the foreground provides a strong sense of perspective, so draw it as a set of converging lines.

**3** ▶ Add in the fine details, checking that doors and windows are in proportion to the size of the buildings.

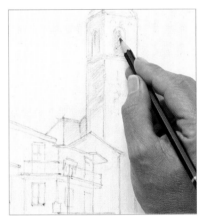

### The Bell Tower

*This simple pencil drawing has been constructed as a series of simple blocks and shapes that provide the basic substance of the drawing. The main features were all measured before they were drawn onto the paper. Then they were developed into more detailed structures once the proportions and balance of the picture had been established.*

**The three-dimensional** appearance of these buildings creates a strong sense of depth.

**Individual features** have been measured carefully so that they have the right proportions.

**This wall** has been constructed with lines that tend toward one another to give a powerful sense of perspective.

*James Horton*

### Materials

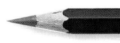

*4B pencil*

### PLUMB LINE

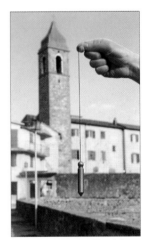

A plumb line – a small weight on the end of a piece of string that gives a true vertical line – is vital if you need to check how straight and balanced a building actually is.

# BUILDINGS & ARCHITECTURE

THE GREAT ADVANTAGE of drawing buildings is that they are permanent and stationary, so you can take your time to study the subject. Perspective – how an object with regular sides appears to diminish toward a vanishing point and so create a feeling of recession – is one of the most important elements to grasp if you want to draw a convincing architectural study. It is also vital to get proportions right so that the space occupied by windows and doors is in relation to the overall size of the building and the scale of any ornate or interesting features is exact. Modern buildings are usually quite simple in appearance, while older buildings such as cathedrals are likely to be more ornate and will adhere to classical rules of proportion. Watch for the changing effects of light on architecture as it can create interesting patterns of highlights and shadows, and try to describe a variety of textural surfaces to enliven your drawing.

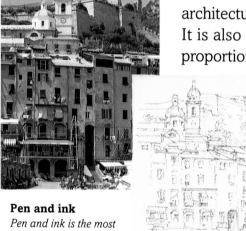

**Pen and ink**
*Pen and ink is the most suitable medium to use for drawing buildings, as you can exploit the fine lines it gives to capture busy scenes or small details.*

### Picking the right location
Once you have chosen an interesting building to draw, pick a quiet spot where you can easily view the whole structure – preferably at an angle so that you can draw more than one side of the building and give it a greater sense of solidity. The eye level from which you view it is also worth thinking about, especially if you want to emphasize the height of an imposing building.

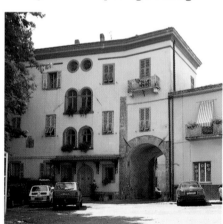

**Simplifying details**
*You can easily simplify the buildings you draw if there are too many extraneous details, or omit unsightly objects such as parked cars. Such details can look too prominent and may compete unnecessarily with the architectural design.*

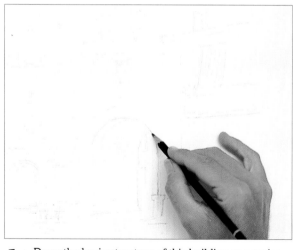

1 ▲ Draw the basic structure of this building as a series of simple geometric shapes with a pencil on smooth Ingres paper; handmade paper is too rough and uneven when you start using pen and ink. This building is slightly curved at the top, so look for the way the light accentuates these different angles.

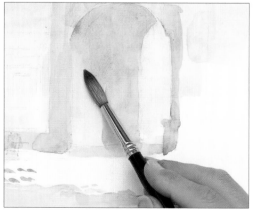

2 ◀ Mix up a pale brown wash of watercolor and apply it liberally over the drawing with a large sable brush to suggest the general tones of the building. Mix a deeper wash for areas with the darkest shadows, such as the overhanging trees to the left and the inside of the archway.

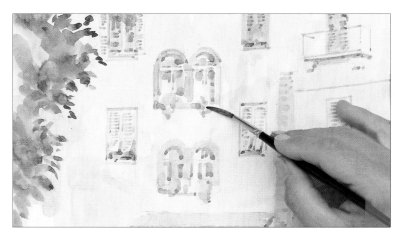

3 ◀ When the wash of color has dried, use a small sable brush to depict the textures and details of the building with a darker brown, describing the brickwork and the wooden slats of the window shutters with gentle dabs of color. Sable brushes, with their finely tapered points and ability to retain paint, allow you to draw far more precisely than other types of brushes.

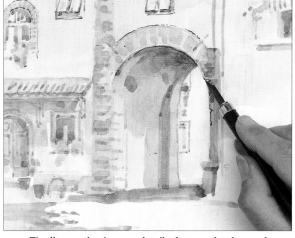

4 ▶ For the finest details, use a brown sepia ink and a dip pen with a steel nib. Draw in the ornate wrought ironwork of the balcony carefully, trying not to put too much pressure on the nib – any heavy lines will detract from the delicate quality of the pen work.

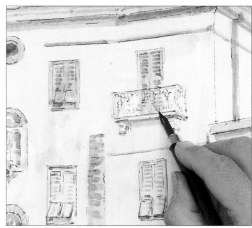

5 ▲ Finally, emphasize any details that need to be made more prominent with the dip pen and sepia ink. The color of this ink serves to enhance rather than detract from the brown watercolor wash. Remember to select only those details that interest you or heighten the characteristic design of the building.

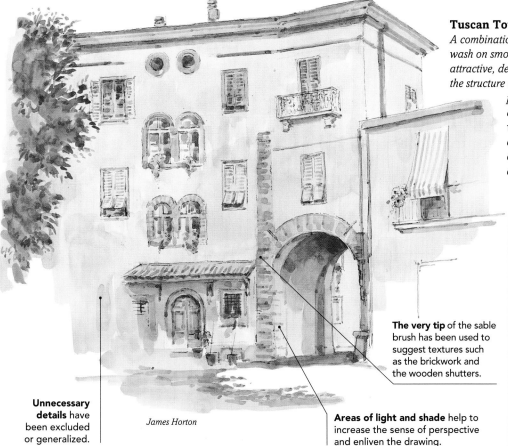

James Horton

**Tuscan Town House**

*A combination of pen and ink and watercolor wash on smooth paper turn this drawing into an attractive, detailed study. The artist has drawn the structure of the building accurately, noting the proportions of individual features and achieving a strong sense of perspective while ignoring details such as the TV antenna on the roof and the parked cars in front. This helps to give the drawing a timeless quality.*

**The very tip** of the sable brush has been used to suggest textures such as the brickwork and the wooden shutters.

**Unnecessary details** have been excluded or generalized.

**Areas of light and shade** help to increase the sense of perspective and enliven the drawing.

### Materials

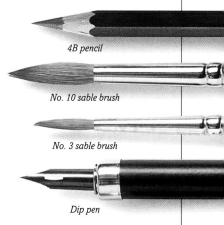

*4B pencil*

*No. 10 sable brush*

*No. 3 sable brush*

*Dip pen*

# INTERIORS & EXTERIORS

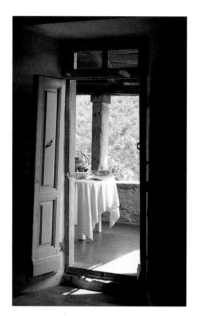

THE MOST MODEST INTERIOR or garden can provide plenty of inspiration for an artist, particularly if the scene is familiar. The advantage of working in such immediate surroundings is that you can look for unusual shapes and interesting spatial relationships in simple objects such as chairs or tables. Combining an interior scene with an exterior view beyond can add an extra dimension to a work and prove a great challenge, particularly in terms of describing the contrasting quality of light inside and out. Select the amount of information you draw in each area to give a balanced composition.

**The changing quality of light**
*The natural light that permeates interiors has a very different quality from that of light outdoors. A variety of suffused rays and deeper tones gives interiors a mellow, quiet atmosphere that provides an effective visual contrast with the strong, even light of outdoors.*

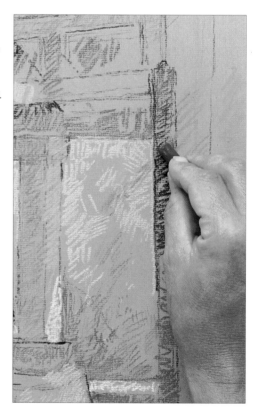

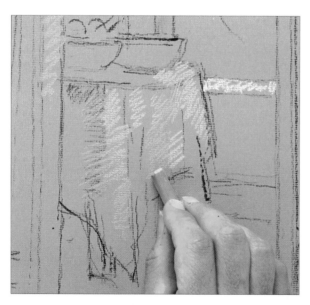

1 ◀ Look for the rich, vivid colors of the view outside and the cool, muted tones of the interior. Sketch the scene in charcoal on mid-toned brown Ingres paper and then apply pale pastel tones to the tablecloth.

2 ▶ Contrast the pale pastels with deep purple and black on the door frame, using a hatching technique. The fine lines of color should appear to blend together optically.

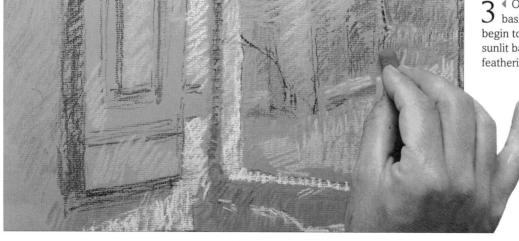

3 ◀ Once you have decided on the basic areas of warm and cool color, begin to overlay the pale colors of the sunlit balcony with richer tones. Use a feathering technique to apply a strong pink over the pale mauve of the balcony floor. This combination of colors should produce a lively, sparkling effect. If you are at all unsure about using a particular pastel color on the toned paper, try it out first on a corner to see how it looks.

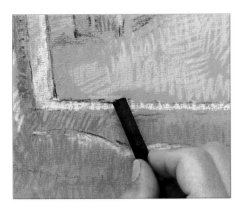

**4** ◀ Emphasize the contrast between the balcony and the interior by drawing dark lines of charcoal in the deepest shadows of the doorway.

**5** ▶ The interior is full of hazy, reflected light – light that bounces off objects in full sunlight. The angled ceiling above the doorway gives off this soft, shimmering light, so use a pale pink tone to draw it.

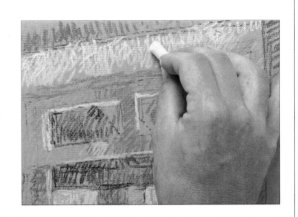

**6** ▶ Finally, rework the fruit on the table with the brightest pastel colors. Then balance the strong hues of the still life by accentuating the details of the doorway with charcoal. Try to keep the background undefined and rather pale to increase the sense of distance beyond the balcony.

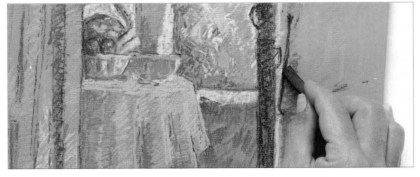

### Main materials

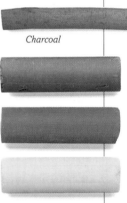

*Charcoal*

*Pastel selection for interior*

### Still Life on a Balcony

*This drawing is built up of color contrasts – with bright, vibrant pastels describing the scene outdoors and darker, more subdued hues evoking the shady interior. This pattern of highlights and shadows sets up a series of strong tonal values through the drawing, which also gives a good sense of aerial perspective. The doorway effectively frames the whole composition and leads the eye up easily to the active focal point of the fruit on the balcony.*

**Pastel marks** have been left unblended so that the drawing has a sharp clarity.

**Bright pastel colors,** either pale or strong in tone, have been used for areas in sunlight.

**The contrast** between the light balcony and the dark interior increases the sense of atmosphere and the aerial perspective, or depth, in the drawing.

*Pastel selection for exterior*

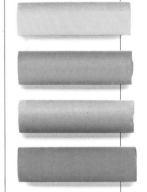

### KEEPING YOUR WORK CLEAN

Pastels and chalks generate a fine powder as you work with them, so use a sheet of paper to lean your hand on as you draw. This technique is also useful with lead pencils.

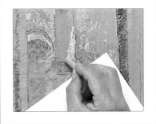

*James Horton*

# GALLERY OF COMPOSITION

A DRAWING CAN BE ANYTHING from a quick doodle in a sketchbook to a highly finished piece of work, yet composition is an important part of any drawing. Composition relies upon a variety of factors, such as the arrangement of shapes and forms and the degree of tone and color. The more complex a drawing becomes, the more you need to consider how individual elements will interrelate to form a cohesive, interesting whole. An unusual viewpoint or angled composition can also produce an engaging work. You may find, after starting a drawing, that you want to explore areas beyond the existing confines of the paper, so add an extra sheet to develop the work into a larger composition.

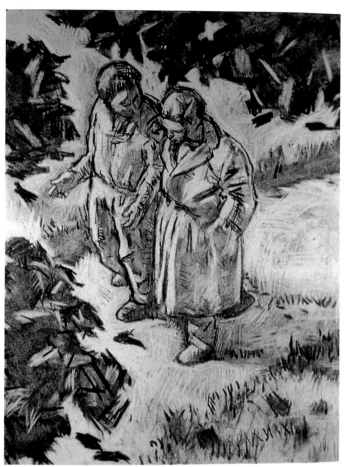

**Thomas Newbolt,**
***Study for the Bandstand III*** *24 x 18 in (61 x 46 cm)*
*In this charcoal drawing the artist has used an ingenious vantage point – from a tree – so that he almost spies on the figures walking below him. As a composition, the drawing is simple but dynamic, with the figures held carefully in place by the diagonal path and the foliage of the tree that frames them.*

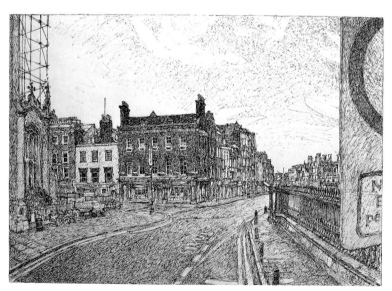

**Jon Harris, *King's Parade*** *22 x 30 in (56 x 76 cm)*
*This work has an extraordinary abundance of lines and marks, which the artist built up using a technical pen while actually sitting in the street. The powerful perspective that characterizes this composition is exaggerated by the road that engulfs the foreground and then converges rapidly to a vanishing point in the distance. The large, dissected road sign dominating the right of the picture increases the immediacy of the composition and gives it a less structured feel. A network of crosshatched marks helps give the picture tone and texture.*

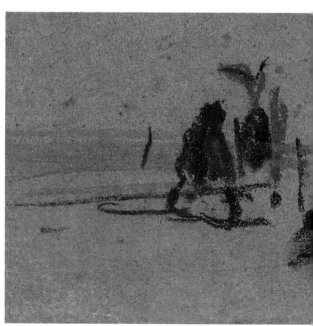

**Jane Stanton,**
***Behind the Scoreboard*** *10 x 14 in (25 x 36 cm)*
*This drawing is one of a series the artist made while sitting behind a cricket scoreboard. Although our attention is immediately drawn to the two seated figures, the artist is also fascinated by the shapes within the room – the intersecting lines of the walls, the repeated image of the doors, and the overhanging cupboards. By placing the figures at an angle, she intensifies our interest and heightens the sense of drama in the scene.*

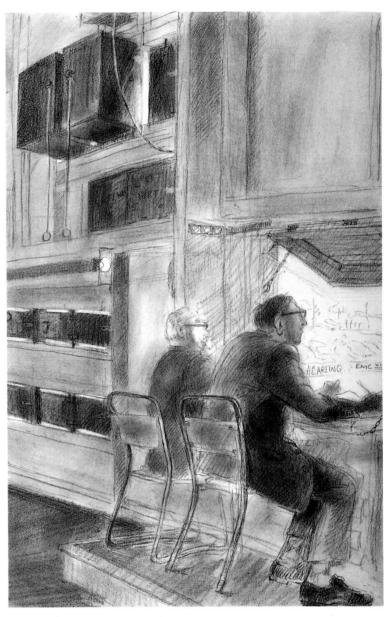

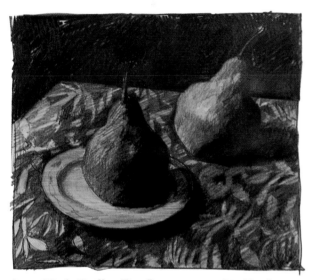

**Anne-Marie Butlin,** *Two Pears* *10 x 12 in (25 x 30 cm)*
This carefully thought out composition transforms a deceptively simple still life into a fascinating study. Viewed from a close angle, the edge of the table that cuts across the picture divides the composition in two so that our attention on the fruit is even more intense. The uneasy positioning of the pears also implies that the artist has sought to generate a certain degree of tension in this picture.

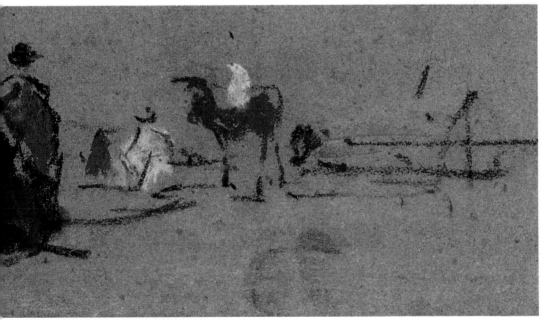

**Boudin,** *Beach Scene,*
***Late* 19th century**

*11½ x 28½ in (29 x 72 cm)*
*This delightful pastel captures the fun of people relaxing on a beach. Boudin has deliberately chosen a long, thin format to reinforce the sensation of gazing out at an endless stretch of coastline. The impressionistic suggestion of figures and shapes in colored pastels gives a spacious, indistinct feel to the drawing so that the scene appears to exist beyond the confines of the toned paper.*

# DRAWING NATURAL FORMS

Drawing natural forms tends to be a genre of its own, since it requires an investigative approach to record precisely and in detail the appearance and workings of an animal or a plant. You need to work methodically to capture the particular characteristics of your subject, rather than applying your own artistic interpretation. Select a medium that is sympathetic to the quality of the object – a bold medium for vigorous drawing and the clean lines of pen and ink for more exacting work.

*Beachcombing is one of the best ways of finding interesting material to draw.*

## Crustaceans

Crustaceans are fascinating to look at, and the "mechanics" of a creature such as this lobster are intriguing. The longer you examine how the different joints are connected and the effects of the hard shell reflecting the light, the more realistic your drawing will be. Use a pencil first to establish the essential shape and features of the lobster before you move on to the permanent medium of pen and ink.

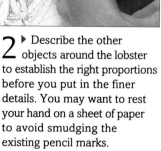

**1** ▶ Arrange the lobster and sea shells in a corner where they can be left to enable you to take your time studying them. Sketch in the basic shape of the lobster with light, gestural strokes on smooth watercolor paper, using a pencil with a sharpened point.

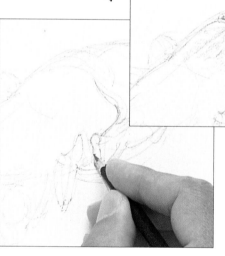

**2** ▶ Describe the other objects around the lobster to establish the right proportions before you put in the finer details. You may want to rest your hand on a sheet of paper to avoid smudging the existing pencil marks.

**3** ◀ With a medium-sized sable brush and a wash of pale yellow, begin to build up the form of the lobster. Apply the watercolor sparingly if you are worried about over-emphasizing any aspect of the work at this stage.

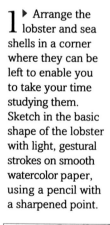

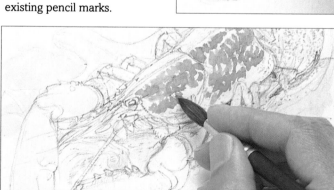

**4** ▲ When the first wash of watercolor has dried, apply a scarlet-brown wash to the main body of the lobster in a series of dabs to echo the appearance of its mottled shell. The springy hairs of the sable brush should give you good control as you paint.

5 ▸ Lightly shade areas of the background with a thin wash of dark brown to give a sense of depth to the drawing and push the form of the lobster forward.

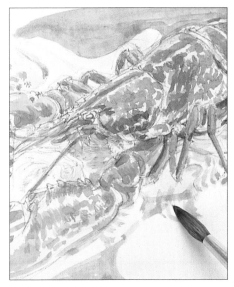

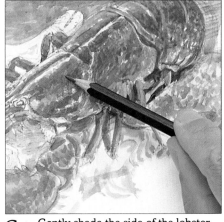

### Materials

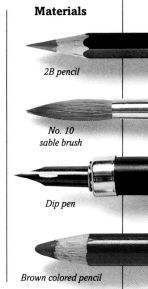

*2B pencil*

*No. 10 sable brush*

*Dip pen*

*Brown colored pencil*

6 ▴ Gently shade the side of the lobster shell with the pencil to build up a series of dark tones. This should help give the image a three-dimensional appearance.

7 ◂ Use a dip pen and sepia ink to redefine the shape and details of the lobster. Accentuate any shadowed areas with thick, dark lines, and highlights with thin, faint lines of ink. Hatched marks drawn in the darkest shadows will also push the image forward.

8 ◂ Deepen the tones of the shell and claws with a dark brown colored pencil. The pencil marks will also add texture to the drawing and help break up any areas of paint that look a little flat.

### Lobster
*The artist has taken his time studying this lobster, and the result is a beautiful and meticulous drawing with a wealth of detail. The layers of color and texture have been applied carefully to give the lobster a powerful sense of form, while the clean, crisp lines of ink define particular features that turn this drawing into a fascinating reference work.*

**Layers of watercolor** have been built up into a series of subtle tones that mold the form of the lobster effectively.

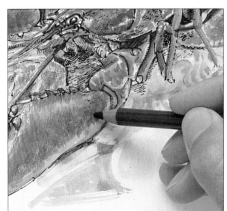

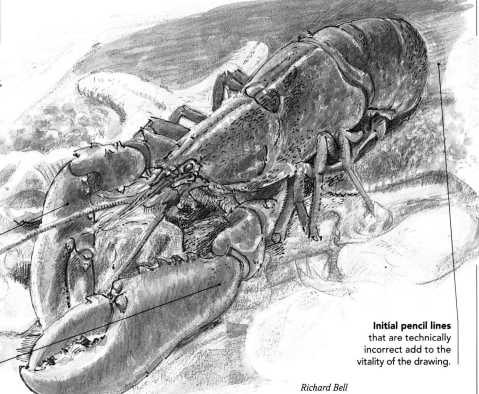

**A colored pencil** breaks up the flat areas of watercolor and provides texture.

**Initial pencil lines** that are technically incorrect add to the vitality of the drawing.

*Richard Bell*

# L ANDSCAPES

D RAWING LANDSCAPES is a relatively recent development in art, and it was not until the eighteenth century that the changing effects of light and weather on a landscape became such popular subject matter. It is always essential to be aware of the passage of the sun across a scene, as the definition of individual features and the length of shadows can change dramatically. Perhaps the greatest problem when you are drawing a landscape is choosing which features to include and which to leave out. A viewfinder is the best way of selecting one view from a broad panorama. Watercolor is one of the most suitable mediums to use for drawing landscapes – it enables you to capture the transient effects of the weather quickly.

1 ▶ Use a viewfinder to select an appealing composition. With a pencil, measure the proportions of the hill village and draw it in a series of blocks and triangles on rough watercolor paper. The slightly off-center positioning of the village creates an unusual composition and the vegetation surrounding it can be sketched in gradually to balance out the drawing.

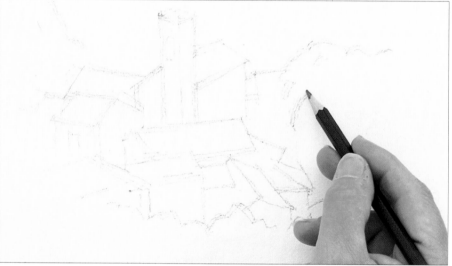

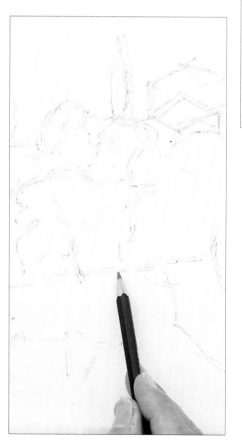

2 ◀ Look for features in the foreground and middle ground, such as trees or a sloping hill, that give a sense of perspective; a diagonal line on the left helps lead the eye up to the village. Keep the landscape on the same scale as the village by measuring the different features carefully.

3 ▶ When you are happy with the scale of the composition, add some watercolor with a small sable brush to capture the effect of sunlight on the buildings. Use a wash of warm red for rooftops and cool purples for shadows.

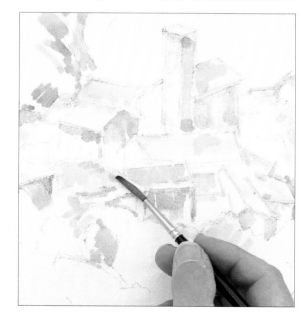

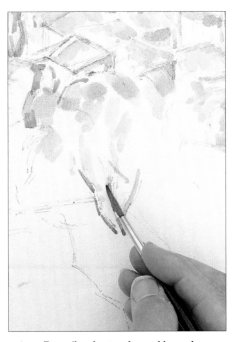

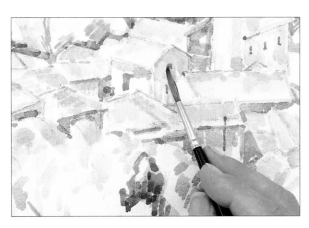

5 ▶ Add some yellow highlights for buildings that catch the sunlight and draw in any small details, such as windows and doors, to give each building more of a three-dimensional form.

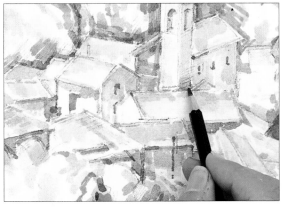

4 ▲ Describe the trunks and branches of the trees in the foreground with the sable brush and a pale brown wash. Apply the wash lightly to retain the clarity of line, and lift out any mistakes you may make with a piece of paper towel.

6 ◀ Use the pencil to suggest any shadows that are cast by the bell tower. Angle the pencil slightly so that you can gently shade the darkest areas. If the surrounding landscape still appears rather sparse, add more light, gestural strokes of watercolor to strengthen the composition of the drawing.

**Mediterranean Hillside**
*The paper used for this drawing was quite absorbent, so that every mark made with the sable brush was linear and decisive, reinforcing the simplicity of the initial pencil drawing. The repeated watercolor marks also help to give the sensation of a large expanse of hillside stretching out around the small village.*

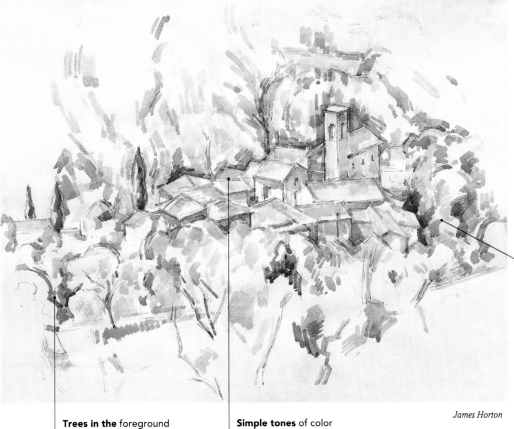

**The surrounding** vegetation is merely suggested, rather than described in detail.

**Trees in the** foreground are used as identifiable landmarks and give a sense of perspective to the drawing.

**Simple tones** of color on the buildings evoke the sensation of bright sunshine hitting the village at an angle.

*James Horton*

**Materials**

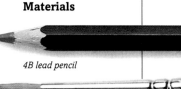

*4B lead pencil*

*No. 4 sable brush*

# GALLERY OF NATURAL FORMS & LANDSCAPES

DRAWING NATURAL FORMS has often brought artist and scientist together. Many of Leonardo's drawings, for example, work equally well as drawings from life and as detailed scientific studies. Until the advent of photography in the mid-nineteenth century, drawing was used to illustrate all kinds of different subjects – resulting in a combination of images that were beautiful to look at and filled with relevant information. Drawing is all about the way we perceive the world around us, which is perhaps why artists turn so readily to landscapes and natural objects as a source of inspiration. Some interesting landscapes contain not only natural features; manmade buildings in a landscape can often strike a balance with the natural forms around them so that they seem to be subsumed into the environment.

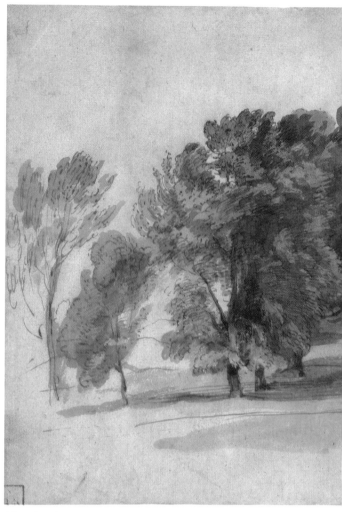

**Van Dyck,** *Study of Trees, late* **1630s** *8 x 9½ in (20 x 24 cm)*
*The feathery texture of the trees in this lyrical pen and ink drawing illustrate Van Dyck's concern for a stylistic interpretation of his subject rather than the identification of particular trees.*

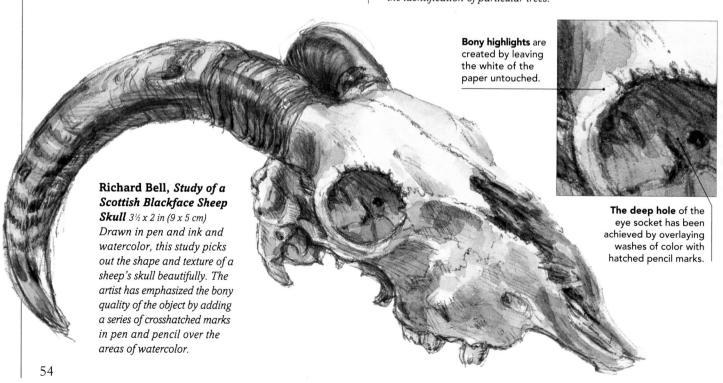

**Bony highlights** are created by leaving the white of the paper untouched.

**Richard Bell,** *Study of a Scottish Blackface Sheep Skull* *3½ x 2 in (9 x 5 cm)*
*Drawn in pen and ink and watercolor, this study picks out the shape and texture of a sheep's skull beautifully. The artist has emphasized the bony quality of the object by adding a series of crosshatched marks in pen and pencil over the areas of watercolor.*

**The deep hole** of the eye socket has been achieved by overlaying washes of color with hatched pencil marks.

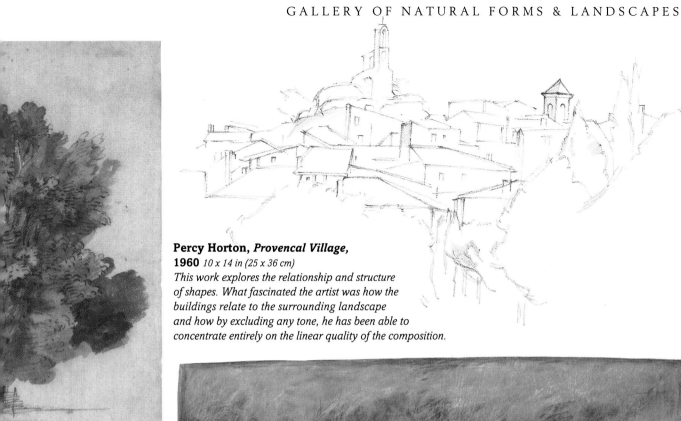

**Percy Horton, *Provencal Village,***
**1960** *10 x 14 in (25 x 36 cm)*
*This work explores the relationship and structure*
*of shapes. What fascinated the artist was how the*
*buildings relate to the surrounding landscape*
*and how by excluding any tone, he has been able to*
*concentrate entirely on the linear quality of the composition.*

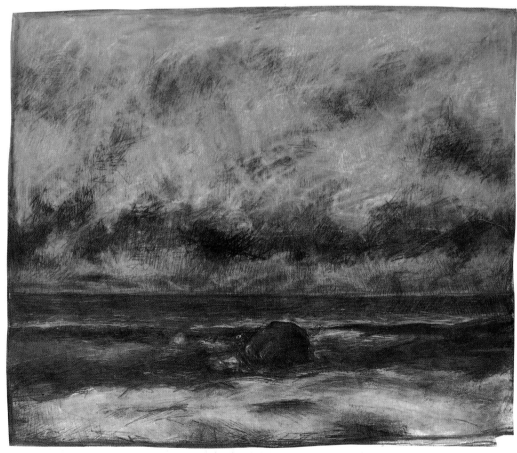

**Paul Lewin, *Seascape (After***
***Courbet)*** *25 x 28 in (64 x 71 cm)*
*In this drawing the artist, rather*
*like Van Dyck, has concentrated*
*on a personal interpretation of*
*a natural scene. He has applied*
*pastel and charcoal vigorously to*
*develop a dramatic sense of mood*
*and atmosphere. Although the*
*picture has a low horizon point,*
*the sky is brought alive with strong*
*color and texture to form a*
*surface full of movement. This*
*work illustrates how a landscape*
*can be used as a springboard*
*for a personal vision.*

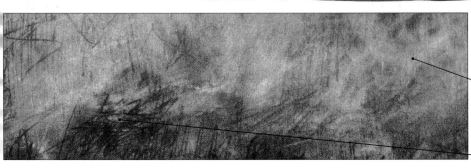

**The lack of fine detail** gives this
seascape an expressionistic feel,
which is heightened by the
limited use of color.

**The dark, moody atmosphere** of
this drawing has been heightened
by a series of deep tones and
heavy crosshatching.

# FIGURES & DRAPERY

CLOTHES CAN DISGUISE and distort the real shape of our bodies, so it is important to understand how material behaves as it falls in folds around a figure. The simplest way to draw a clothed figure is to work out the proportions of the body first and draw it as a series of simple forms, ignoring the flowing shapes made by the drapery. Once you are satisfied with the shape of the figure, you can begin to explore the way the material hangs from particular areas of the body. Don't overwork the folds and gathers of the drapery or the image will look stiff and unnatural.

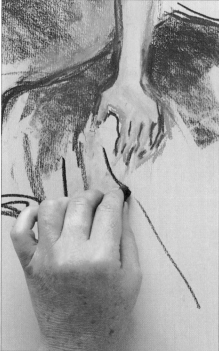

### Sketching figures

People always make engaging studies. A good way to gain confidence in drawing people is with a sketchbook: make quick sketches of seated figures on buses or trains and note how their clothes hang and serve to accentuate the way they sit.

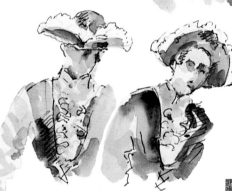

### Moving figures

*If you draw repeated studies of a moving figure, use a fast medium such as pencil or pen and watercolor to capture the most interesting features: look for the way their clothes behave as they twist and turn.*

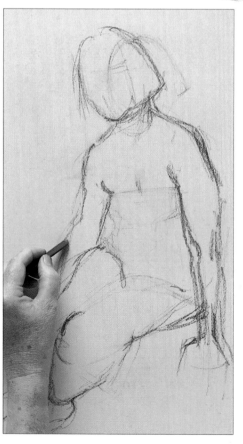

1 ◀ The folds made by drapery create interesting patterns on and around this figure. Draw in the proportions of the woman first with charcoal on lightly toned pastel paper, reducing the image to a series of simple shapes. Repeat lines or change the angle of the head until you have an accurate rendering of the figure.

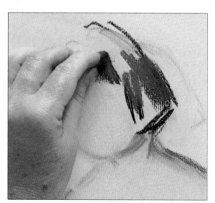

2 ▲ Loosely block in the essential features and skin coloring of the figure with soft pastels until you have achieved a reasonable human likeness. Then concentrate on describing the varying rhythms and tones of the different materials.

3 ▲ Draw in the deep folds created by the drapery thrown over the seat, looking to see how it hangs and catches the light. You will need to use a wide range of green pastels to re-create the strong lighting effects, so first establish the shapes of the drapery in one color.

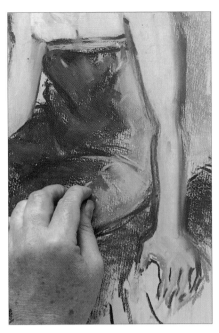

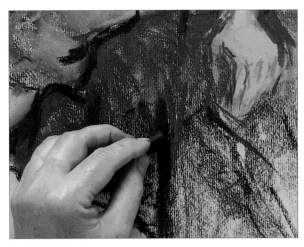

4 ◀ Build up the tones of the woman's sarong, using dark colors for the deepest creases that help to shape her body. Then pick out the red pattern of the cloth and observe how its regularity is disrupted by folds and contours.

5 ▶ Use a deep blue pastel and charcoal for areas of fabric that cast the strongest shadows. This will give the material an intense, heavy feel and a sense of depth.

**Main materials**

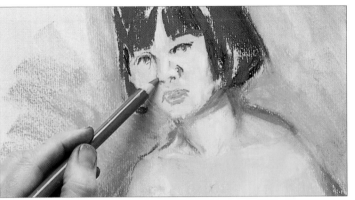

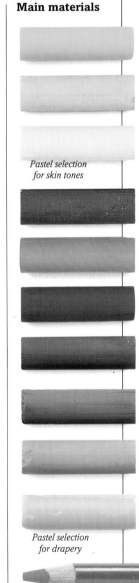

*Pastel selection for skin tones*

6 ▶ Draw in the finer details of the figure with a pastel pencil: a slightly harder version of a soft pastel in a pencil format. This will allow you to work more precisely on smaller areas such as the face, capturing the final highlights and emphasizing any particular features.

**Malaysian Woman in a Sarong**
*This richly colored study of a figure gives a strong visual description of the nature of drapery and the way it can echo and enhance the rhythms of the human body. The blended pastels on her sarong illustrate how the light strikes her body and gives it form, while layers of dark pastel on the bench fabric create the effect of a heavier, thicker cloth falling to the ground.*

**The shape** of this figure is simple, yet strong enough to give a solid image on which to draw the hanging material.

**The irregularity** of the red pattern helps to identify the contours of the body and creases in the material.

**Bold lines** of dark color have been used for the deepest folds of cloth while the lightest tints pick up the direction of the strong light source.

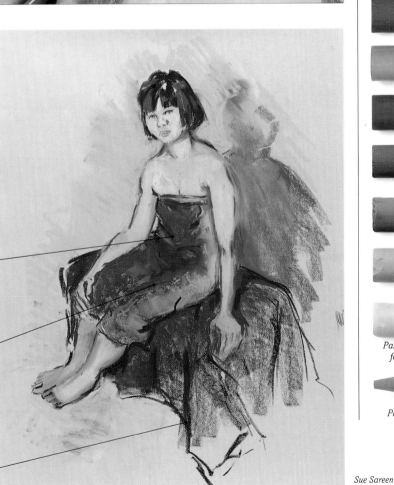

*Pastel selection for drapery*

*Pastel pencil*

*Sue Sareen*

# LIFE DRAWING

THE HUMAN BODY is generally thought to contain every aspect of form, visual complexity, and subtlety that an artist will encounter. Drawing a human figure regularly will help you to improve your powers of observation and drawing skills, but it is often hard for artists to find people willing to devote their time to sit as models. By joining a life-drawing class you can take your time studying figures and gleaning different ideas and techniques from observing other artists. While you should learn to pay attention to the anatomical proportions of the human body, a life-drawing class will also allow you the freedom to express a mood in the way a model sits or stands, or a certain characteristic feature in their personality.

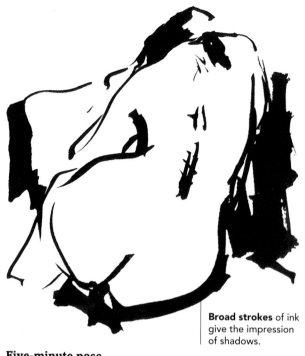

**Broad strokes** of ink give the impression of shadows.

**Five-minute pose**
*This decisive yet eloquent study of a woman's back shows how a few expressive lines and the minimum of detail can create a convincing image. The study was drawn with a Chinese brush and ink, which encourages a lyrical style full of control.*

## The classroom

A life-drawing class provides a regular, disciplined period where the problems and complexities of the human figure can be tackled.

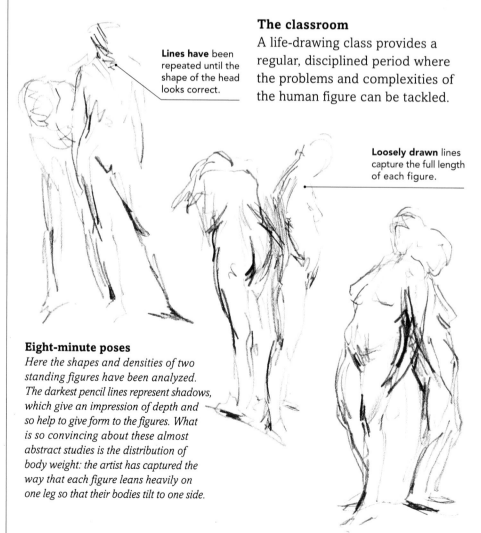

**Lines have** been repeated until the shape of the head looks correct.

**Loosely drawn** lines capture the full length of each figure.

**Eight-minute poses**
*Here the shapes and densities of two standing figures have been analyzed. The darkest pencil lines represent shadows, which give an impression of depth and so help to give form to the figures. What is so convincing about these almost abstract studies is the distribution of body weight: the artist has captured the way that each figure leans heavily on one leg so that their bodies tilt to one side.*

In order to get to know the different aspects of a model, it is useful to begin with a series of exercises that test your powers of observation rather than your ability to draw a lifelike figure.

By getting a model to do a series of timed poses, from about five minutes to several hours, you can develop a range of strategies and approaches with which to analyze and interpret the human figure. The quickest drawings, of five minutes or less, require a very swift, gestural style: you have to capture the essence of the model's stance by looking carefully for the strongest shapes and then distilling them into an impressionistic image. The most important aspect of this exercise is to draw the whole length of the figure and not waste time concentrating on incidental details.

Ten- and fifteen- minute poses still demand a certain speed, but they allow you to develop your style beyond the purely gestural. Take this extra time to look for the dynamic angles and planes of the body. Look also for the way that the model's stance affects the distribution of weight through the body, using a plumb line, if necessary, to determine the balance of the figure in relation to a true vertical line. With any short pose it is important to develop the drawing only as far as the time will allow and not to over-emphasize any individual characteristics.

Taking thirty minutes to an hour to draw a figure will give you the chance to develop more intricate aspects of character and study the form of the body in some detail. Work up a series of tones with solid shading or crosshatching and hatching to give the body a sense of depth and volume.

With poses of two hours or more, a different process evolves. The proportions of the body are more significant, so use the size of the head as a basic unit of measurement. The body should be approximately seven and a half times larger than the head. Think also about the light source: enhanced or distorted effects created by the light as it shines from different angles can create a fascinating study. Be aware of the patterns made by shadows across the body and how some areas are totally obscured, while other muscles or features are accentuated by an intense bright light. Describing the surroundings at this stage will help to put the figure in a more realistic context.

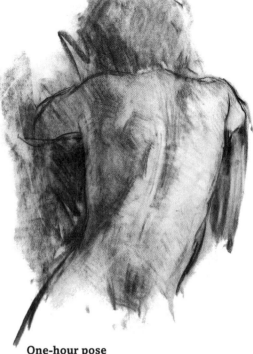

**One-hour pose**
*Here the light hitting the back of the body illuminates some of the many planes and facets of the human figure. Such dips and curves, caused by muscles and bones beneath the skin, are important to depict – they give substance to the study. Although the shading is roughly executed, the effect gives a rugged realism.*

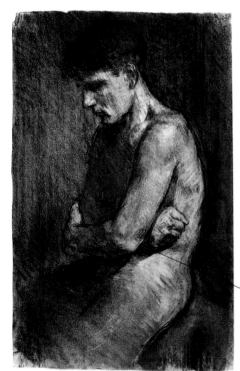

**The contrast** of strong lights and darks gives this drawing atmosphere.

**Two-hour pose**
*With more time to study his personal character, the artist has explored the mood of this man and generated a strong atmosphere of brooding contemplation. The wide range of tonal values drawn in charcoal gives the figure solidity, while the weight of his body pulls downward to give a forceful sense of gravity.*

**Four-hour pose**
*Subtle blending and a powerful perspective give this drawing a sensuous yet controlled feeling. The artist has taken his time modeling the figure, picking out the highlights with care so that the final impression is of a woman bathed in suffused sunlight. The treatment of the bed and the highlights that have been produced with an eraser add to the softness of the scene.*

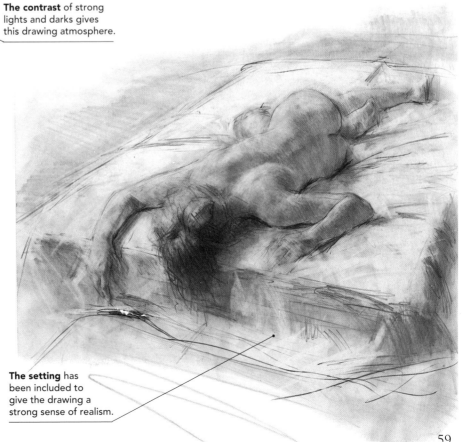

**The setting** has been included to give the drawing a strong sense of realism.

# PORTRAITS

THE NEED TO DEPICT a person's individual characteristics sets portrait drawing apart from figure drawing. The best approach to take when you draw a portrait is to study the construction and form of the head, noting the proportions of particular features in relation to the size of the face. You may wish to experiment with the lighting to create an atmosphere or reflect the mood of the sitter, and such unusual effects may help you look at your subject in a fresh, interesting way. If you need practice capturing a reasonable human likeness, try drawing a self-portrait so that you can work at your own rate of speed.

### Capturing a mood
*Often the medium you use will reflect the mood of the sitter. A bold, heavy drawing in charcoal may signal an angry or defiant mood; a pencil drawing will enable you to describe a range of tones to give dimension to a portrait; a delicate pen and ink drawing can pick up the subtle nuances of a person's character.*

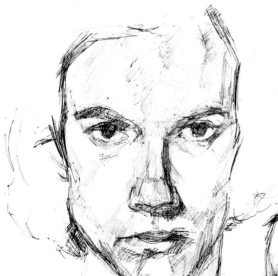

### Lighting
*Lighting can radically affect the appearance of an individual. A full light shining straight onto the face will flatten the features and give you little chance to explore the depth of the head. Light shining on the side of the head creates a more interesting study, but if you want to exaggerate someone's personality or create an unsettling effect, try lighting them from below.*

### Proportions
*To draw a portrait successfully, you need to be able to produce a solid, lifelike image of a head with recognizable features that identify the sitter. Work out the symmetry of the face by dividing it roughly into three equal parts. The top section is from the crown to the brow; the central section is from the brow to the end of the nose; and the bottom section is from the end of the nose to the bottom of the chin. Draw the eyes approximately one eye's width apart, and measure the triangle made by the eyes and the end of the nose. These are important features and define the particular shape of the face most accurately.*

## Self-portrait

Self-portrait studies are a good way to practice drawing human features, although they often portray a rather confrontational gaze as a result of your staring at yourself in the mirror. Select the most essential and interesting features as you draw – if you attempt to capture every detail you may end up with an overworked drawing.

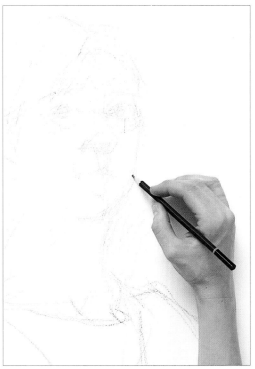

1 ▶ Set up a mirror in a convenient place so that you can see yourself easily and, if possible, where the light will cast shadows for an interesting effect. Sketch the shape of your head and features in pencil on a broad sheet of textured paper, keeping the drawing as large as possible.

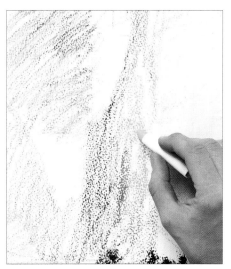

2 ▲ Block in the main areas of the face and hair with oil pastels, applying each color loosely to cover the paper effectively. Oil pastels give a rich, colorful effect and adhere to the paper easily. Use a cloth dipped in turpentine to wipe away mistakes or colors you may want to change.

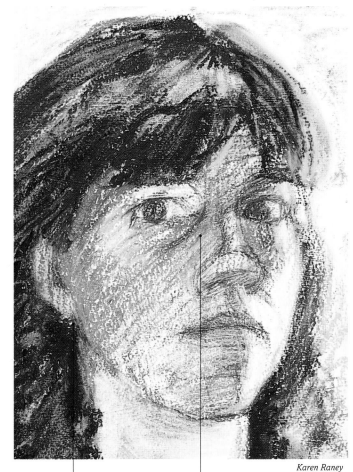

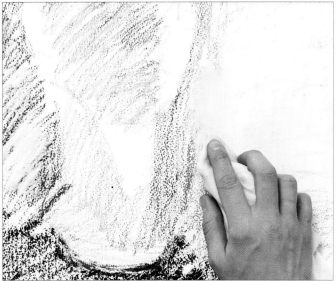

### Self-Portrait Study

*Oil pastels give this self-portrait a richer, deeper effect than ordinary pastels would. The slight transparency of the oil pastels also allows separate lines of overlaid color to create an optical mix. The size of the paper is significant; it gave the artist confidence to draw boldly and capture the strong lighting effects cast across the side of her face.*

Karen Raney

3 ▲ Use a finger or a piece of material to blend pastel marks together if you want to give a smoother texture to some areas of skin. Make sure the pastels are soft so that you can blend them easily on paper.

**Yellows and oranges** have been used for warm lights, and cool mauves and grays for areas in shadow.

**Pastel marks** have been built up in layers to create an optical mix of color.

### Main materials

*4B pencil*

*Oil pastel*

# FIGURES IN A SETTING

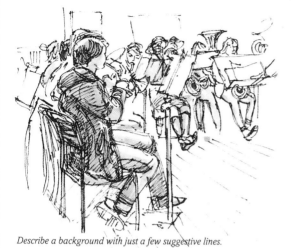

*Describe a background with just a few suggestive lines.*

FIGURES ARE RARELY SEEN in isolation – usually they are situated against a backdrop, either indoors or outside. Invariably the background is a significant element in a drawing, but the most important thing to remember is that you should always relate the figures to their surroundings. The interaction between the two needs to be organized carefully within a composition to give a strong sensation of depth and create a series of spatial relationships. Try to avoid including too much background detail; this will keep the emphasis of the drawing centered on the figures.

### Establishing a focal point

The human eye is similar to a camera lens in that it cannot focus on everything at once, so you will need to work systematically to establish the figure as a focal point first. Then go on to develop the background scene.

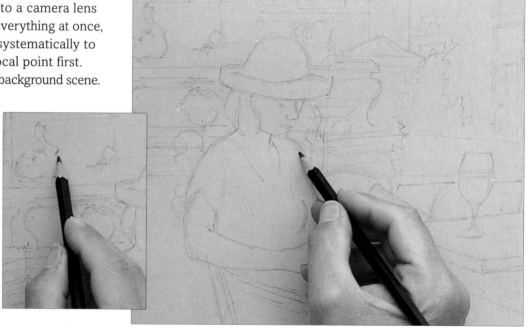

1 ▶ Sketch the figure lightly first in pencil on a toned, semi-rough watercolor paper. Then draw in the fountain and the most prominent features of the buildings. Once you have all the proportions drawn correctly, return to the figure and strengthen the image.

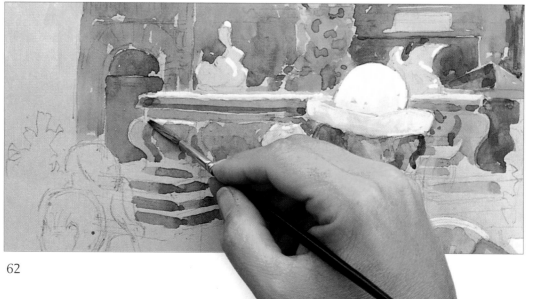

2 ◀ As this café scene is situated outside in a square, the quality of light is much stronger, casting short dark shadows and producing bright highlights. Mix some cool washes of watercolor for areas of the fountain and buildings that are in shadow and apply them with a small sable brush.

3 ▶ Represent the way the light defines the form of this figure with dark transparent washes for shadows and white gouache for the highlights. White gouache is essential for describing strong light and pale colors if you are working on toned paper. Redefine details, such as the hat, with a pencil. These subtle lines will give a better sense of form and shape and help push the figure farther into the foreground.

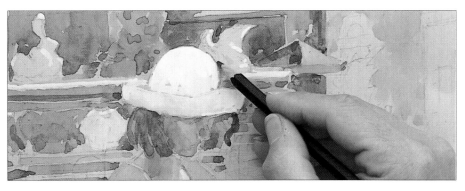

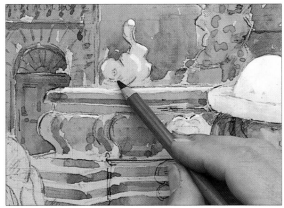

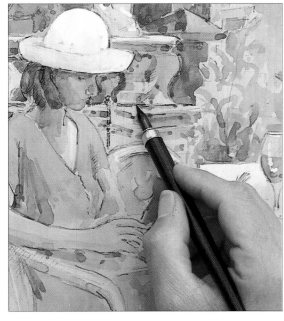

5 ◀ Use a dip pen and brown ink to draw in the final details, redefining any pencil marks that may have been covered by the washes of color.

4 ▲ Use a charcoal pencil delicately to shade small features such as the stonework on the fountain. This refined form of charcoal retains the dark, heavy quality of the medium, while the pencil format allows you a greater degree of control and precision.

**Materials**

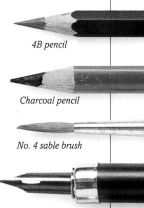

*4B pencil*

*Charcoal pencil*

*No. 4 sable brush*

*Dip pen*

**Town Square**
*This figure and the setting behind her both complement and balance each other; the figure blends into the scene while still looking prominent enough as a focal point. The scale of the background also relates proportionally to the figure and the light cast across the whole scene links individual features in a series of strong tonal contrasts.*

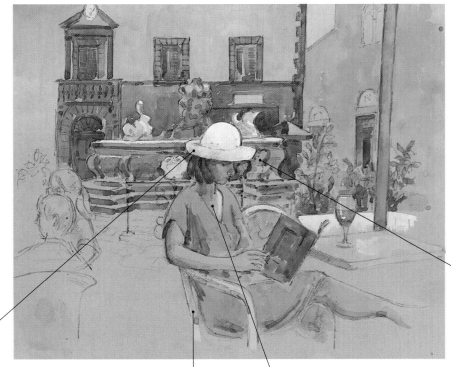

**The strong** sense of perspective gives the impression of a large area of space between the figure and the fountain.

**The shape** of the girl's hat provides an interesting feature against the fountain in the background.

*James Horton*

**Opaque highlights** are used to give a feeling of hot, bright light, while dark, transparent hues describe the short shadows of early afternoon.

**Our attention** focuses primarily on the girl, and then on the different features beyond.

63

# GALLERY OF FIGURES

FIGURES HAVE ALWAYS been a fascinating subject matter for artists; after all, almost everyone is aware of, perhaps even intrigued by, the people around them and how they move and act. To draw figures successfully and understand your subject, you must capture not just the right proportions and shape of a human body, but the character of an individual. Details that may only be subconsciously observed on an everyday level, such as the color of someone's eyes or the way they dress, can be deliberately exaggerated in a drawing to transform the personality of a figure and emphasize their character. What all of these artists have achieved in their work is a convincing portrayal of human life that encapsulates each individual succinctly.

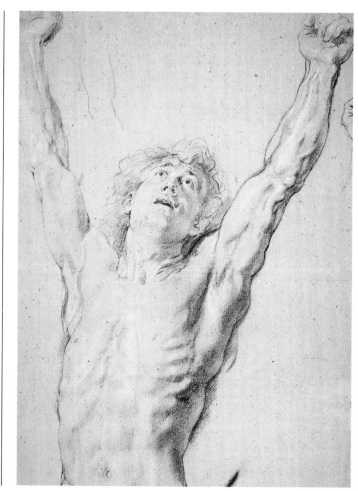

**Rubens, *Study of a Crucified Man,***
**c.1614-15** *21 x 14½ in (53 x 37 cm)*
*This work in brown chalk is typical of the many studies Rubens would have made in preparation for a painting. Rubens used the drawing to familiarize himself with every aspect of this man's torso, bringing out the complexities of human form with remarkable subtlety. He describes the contours of the body and the muscles on the chest with precise yet evocative lines. His use of brown chalk is actually quite sparing and understated, though the tone of the paper and white chalk highlights generate a strong feeling of solidity.*

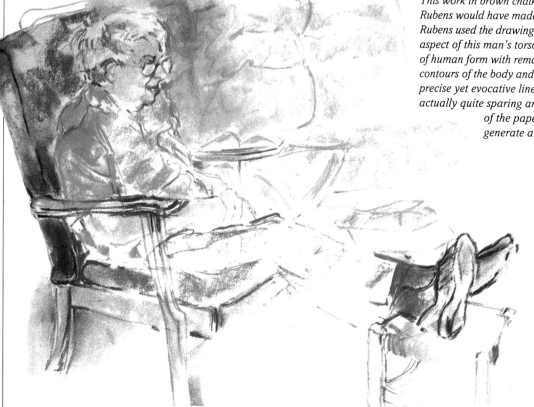
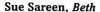

**Sue Sareen, *Beth***
*23 x 16 in (58 x 41 cm)*
*This portrait brings out the character of the sitter most sensitively. While not making a particularly detailed study, the artist has conveyed the personality of this figure effectively with small details, such as her posture and the position of her feet. The addition of color reinforces the loosely drawn image and accentuates the slumped position of this woman in her chair.*

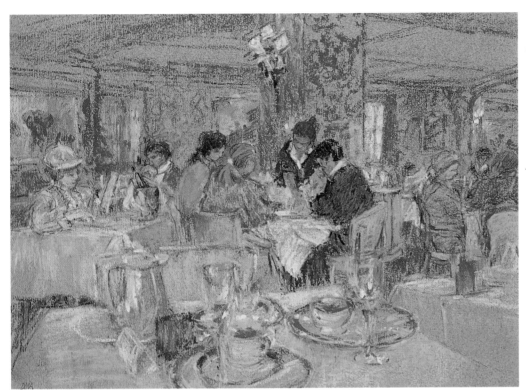

**Diana Armfield, RA,**
*Studying the Menu at Fortnum's, London,*
*17½ x 10½ in (44 x 27cm)*
*In this pastel drawing the artist has cleverly arranged her composition so that the focus of attention is actually on the group of figures in the middle distance, in spite of the spacious foreground. The lack of finished detail in the foreground helps to lead the eye straight to the tables of seated customers, who appear more dominant than they really are. Although these figures are relatively small, their movements have been thoughtfully described and there is even a suggestion of their characters. Most importantly, they appear very much part of their environment, giving the work a strong sense of unity.*

**Norman Blamey, RA,**
*St. Andrew, Fisher of Men* 14 x 9 in (36 x 23 cm)
*This work is a study for a mural; the drawing has been squared up, ready to be transferred onto a wall. The most noticeable aspect of this study is the high viewpoint the artist has chosen. The rapid descent toward the foot, and the arms that appear too long for the body, are caused by an acute foreshortening of the whole figure. Again, Blamey has assiduously explored and studied his figure to create a profoundly fascinating drawing.*

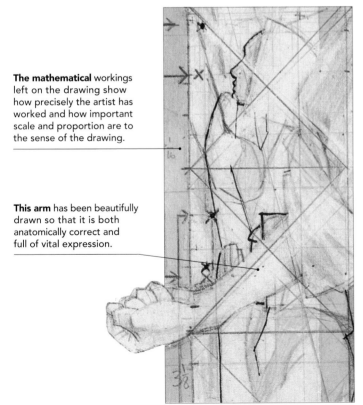

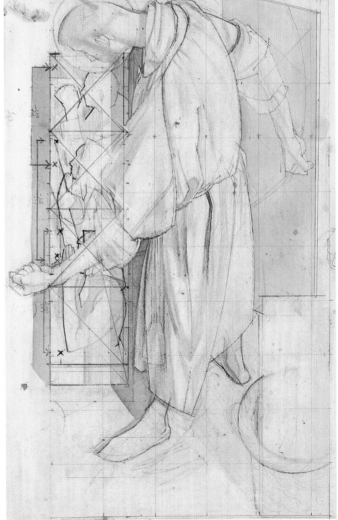

**The mathematical** workings left on the drawing show how precisely the artist has worked and how important scale and proportion are to the sense of the drawing.

**This arm** has been beautifully drawn so that it is both anatomically correct and full of vital expression.

# MOVEMENTS & GESTURES

ONCE YOU HAVE gained confidence drawing people sitting still for you in a controlled environment, try drawing a scene full of movement and vitality. This type of subject matter requires a different approach: you need to be able to memorize a certain amount of information every time you look away from the scene, since it will change constantly.

This process depends upon assessing a fluctuating image and distilling it before you begin to draw. Dancers or animals are good subjects to begin with, as they often repeat movements or gestures, but try to adopt a loose style so that you can capture the essence of an image quickly. Working in this way, your drawings should have a freshness and immediacy that is difficult to achieve in a regulated situation.

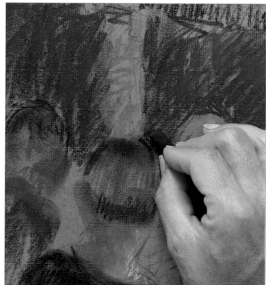

*Study animals such as lions and tigers and notice how they move.*

### Suggesting movement

The speed at which you need to draw a moving image means that you have to be adept at suggesting information and giving clues with the minimum of linear marks and shading. The best media to use for such fast work are those that enable you to cover the paper swiftly, such as watercolor or pastels.

*Dancers, with their ability to move gracefully and powerfully, make fascinating subjects.*

1 ▶ Choose a richly toned blue Ingres paper and capture this atmospheric evening scene on a balcony as quickly as possible with charcoal, reworking any lines swiftly and repeatedly until you are happy with the positioning of the figures.

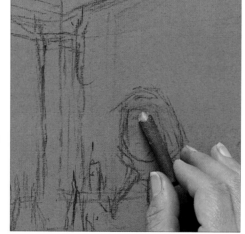

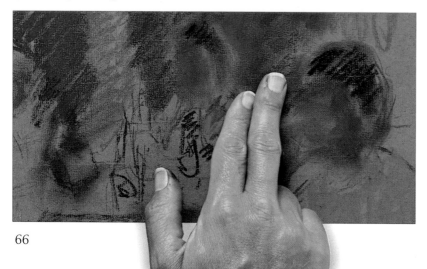

2 ▲ As this scene is full of movement and fleeting impressions, use your imagination to select interesting colors. Note any areas illuminated by the light with a bright orange-yellow pastel and loosely block in the background with deep, rich blues and purples.

3 ◀ To give a more impressionistic, hazy feel to the background, merge the blue and purple pastels by smudging the colors together around each figure with your fingers. Be sure to wash your hands afterward to avoid soiling the drawing.

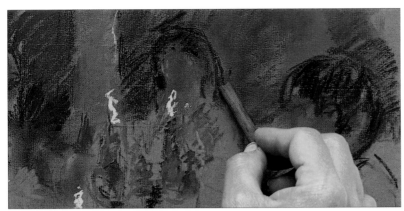

4 ◀ Build up the form of each seated figure with a series of dark tones, using charcoal to redefine any outlines against the dark background. Try to capture the position or stance of the five diners – whether they are resting their elbows on the table, or leaning on the armrest of their chair – rather than attempting to discern facial expressions and small details.

**Main materials**

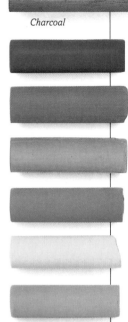

*Charcoal*

*Selection of pastel colors*

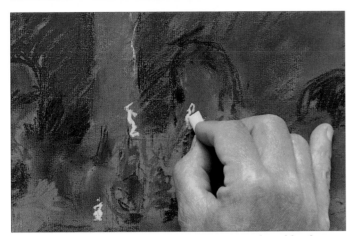

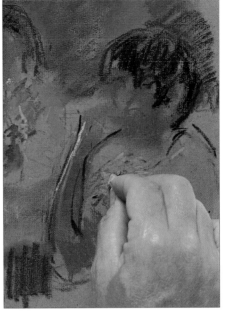

5 ▲ As these figures all face one another around a table, they should be linked by a focal point to give the composition some unity. The bright, magnetic light of the candles in the middle of the table provides this focus, so use a pale pastel color to delineate the flickering flames.

6 ◀ Once you have drawn in the main source of light, use a combination of light green, warm red, and deep yellow to pick out the soft highlights on each figure with loosely hatched marks.

**Evening Meal on a Balcony**

*This night scene is full of fleeting impressions and suggested movement. Only the essential facts have been recorded with a series of gestural lines based upon a few glances and a good visual memory. The lack of attention to detail gives this impressionistic study a shifting rhythm and strong sense of mass.*

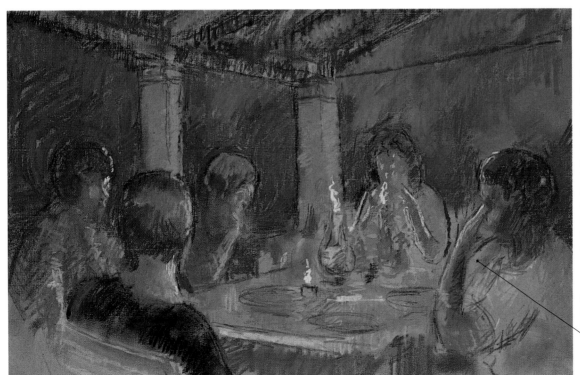

**Soft highlights** help model the form of each figure.

*James Horton*

# DRAWING FOR PAINTING

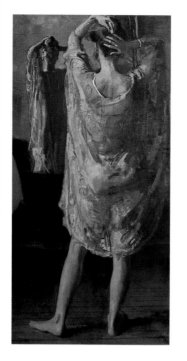

HISTORICALLY, THE MAJORITY of artists' drawings were used solely as studies for later paintings. They were a means to an end rather than an end in themselves. Although drawing now has a much higher status and is accepted as an art form in its own right, drawings are still often used as preparatory studies for other works. A drawing, or a series of drawings, can help you familiarize yourself with your subject matter, investigating, for example, the play of light and assimilating all the information so that you have a precise visual reference as you paint. You can also combine several preparatory drawings into one painting by tracing each individual study and linking them in a strong composition.

**Analyzing the subject**
*In the charcoal work above, the artist John Ward has studied the anatomy of this figure intently so that he can describe her perfectly in "Zandra Rhodes Dress" (right).*

**Collating information**
Making preparatory drawings for a painting is a good method of testing imaginative ideas visually on paper before you commit yourself to canvas. The images below are a mixture of sketches and detailed drawings that were drawn at different times. By scaling the figures down and trying them out in different areas of the room setting, you can establish where they work best to create the most harmonious relationship. If you include several separate drawings in one composition, you can prevent them from looking superimposed by making subtle tonal adjustments as you paint.

**Standing figure**
*Figures should relate to their surroundings, so this image should be scaled to an appropriate size to look realistic within the interior.*

**Interior study**
*The essential details of this scene and the light streaming through the windows provide a good visual reference for a painting.*

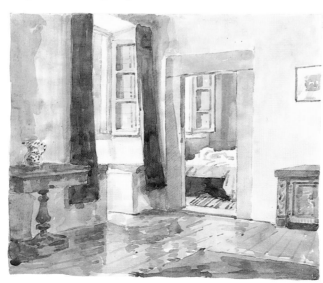

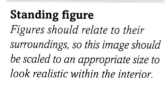

**Seated girl at a window**
*In this pen-and-wash study the light hits the girl from the same direction as it does the standing figure. This creates a clear link between the two.*

## Creating a composition

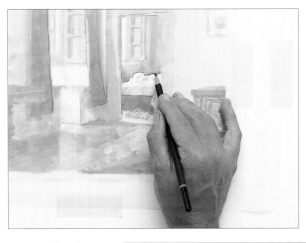

**1** ◀ Begin by copying the basic outlines of the interior study onto tracing paper with a soft pencil, keeping the sketch simple and well defined. Secure the tracing paper with masking tape to prevent it from moving.

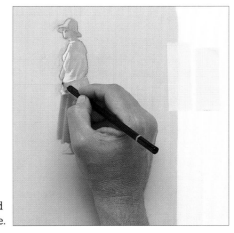

**2** ▶ Scale down any image that is too large. Then trace around the outline of each figure.

**3** ▶ Position the trace of the standing figure over the original interior watercolour study, moving it around until a suitable composition begins to materialize.

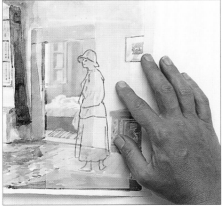

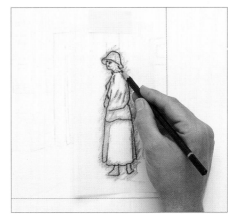

**4** ◀ Transfer all the tracings onto paper, either by heavily shading the opposite side of the tracing paper and drawing the image again, or by using carbon paper.

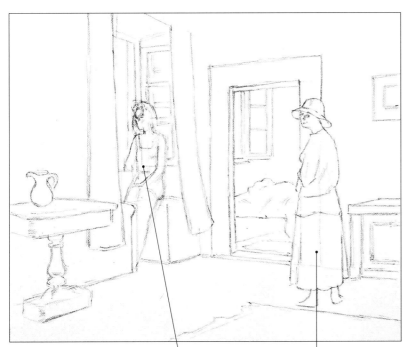

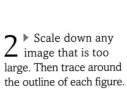

**5** ▲ Once you have drawn in all the images, add the remaining features and details to give a comprehensive scene that can be transferred to canvas.

*James Horton*

### Materials

*6B pencil*

*Tracing paper*

*Masking tape*

### Establishing a Scene
*The artist has successfully placed these two figures in a strong composition in preparation for a detailed painting. Each figure has been accurately scaled to look realistic within the interior setting.*

**Each figure** has been placed in an appropriate part of the setting.

**The most** relevant information has been included to give the composition clarity and interest.

# GLOSSARY

**ABSORBENCY** The degree to which a paper absorbs paint, often due to the amount of surface sizing.

**ACID-FREE PAPER** Paper with a neutral pH that will not darken excessively with age (unlike acidic bleached wood pulp).

**AERIAL PERSPECTIVE** The effect of atmospheric conditions on our perception of the tone and color of distant objects. As objects recede toward the horizon, they appear lighter in tone and more blue.

**BINDING MEDIUM** The substance that holds pigment particles together and attaches them to a surface. Water-soluble gum is used for soft pastels, wax for crayons, and oil for oil pastels.

**BLENDING** A soft, gradual transition from one color or tone to another using either a tortillon or a finger to smudge the colors together.

**BLOCKING IN** Laying in a broad area of color.

**BODY COLOR** Also called gouache. A type of watercolor paint characterized by its opacity.

**BRACELET SHADING** A form of shading in which semi-circular lines are repeatedly drawn close to one another.

**CHARCOAL** Willow, vine, or other twigs partially burned and carbonized in airtight containers.

**COLORED PENCILS** Wax-based crayons in a pencil format and available in a wide selection of colors.

**CONTÉ CRAYON** Chalk-based pastels with a square cross-section; they are midway between soft and hard pastels in texture. Sold in a range of up to 80 colors.

**CROSSHATCHING** Parallel marks overlaid roughly at right angles to another set of parallel marks.

**EASEL** A frame for holding a drawing while the artist works on it. Artists working outdoors tend to use easels of light construction. A good sketching easel allows the drawing to be held securely in any position from horizontal to vertical.

**ELLIPSE** A circle whose apparent height appears to diminish the farther it tilts away from you.

**ERASER** A tool for removing pencil and other marks. In the past artists used rolled bits of bread or feathers. More recently artists have used standard rubber erasers or kneaded erasers, although the new plastic erasers are extremely clean and very versatile.

**FEATHERING** Laying roughly parallel marks, often over a previous area of color, to modify the strength of color or tone.

**FIXATIVE** A resin dissolved in solvent, which is sprayed on to a drawing to fix the particles to the surface.

**FORM** The shape of a three-dimensional object, usually represented by line or tone in a two-dimensional drawing.

**GRANULATION** The mottled effect made by heavy coarse pigments as they settle into the hollows of the paper.

**GRAPHITE PENCIL** Standard pencils are made from a mixture of graphite and clay that is encased in wood. The mixture is initially fired and subsequently impregnated with molten wax. The proportion of graphite to clay varies, and it is this which determines the hardness or softness of the pencil. Graphite has a "silvery" or metallic sheen if used densely.

**GRAPHITE STICK** A thick graphite pencil used for large-scale work that is fixed in a graphite holder rather than encased in cedarwood.

**HATCHING** Making tonal gradations by shading with thin parallel marks.

**HIGHLIGHT** The lightest tone in a drawing.

**HP OR HOT-PRESSED PAPER** Paper with a very smooth surface.

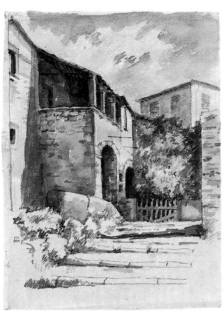

*Watercolor study*

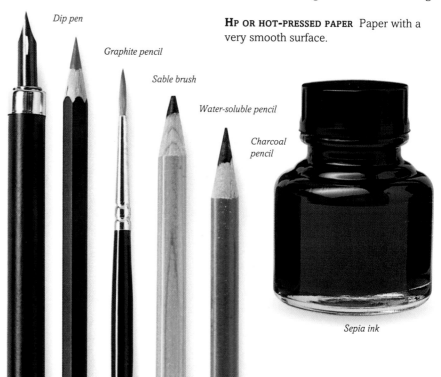

*Dip pen*

*Graphite pencil*

*Sable brush*

*Water-soluble pencil*

*Charcoal pencil*

*Sepia ink*

**HUE** Describes the actual color of an object or substance as it would appear on the color wheel.

**LIFTING OUT** Modifying color and creating highlights by taking color off the paper using an eraser or sponge.

**LINEAR PERSPECTIVE** The method of representing a three-dimensional object on a two-dimensional surface. Linear perspective makes objects appear smaller as they get farther away by means of a geometric system of measurement.

**MODELING** Describing the form of a solid object using solid shading or linear marks.

**MONOCHROMATIC** Drawn or painted in shades of one color.

**NOT OR COLD-PRESSED PAPER** Paper with a fine grain or semi-rough surface.

**OAK GALL INK** Ink made by crushing and boiling oak galls. The galls are formed by parasitic insects living off oak trees and tend to appear in autumn.

**OIL PASTEL** Pastel bound by oil as opposed to gum. The oil gives this type of pastel a slight transparency and a strong adherence to the support. It comes in a less extensive range of colors than soft pastels.

**OPAQUE COLOR** *See* Body color.

**OPTICAL MIX** When a color is arrived at by the visual effect of overlaying or abutting distinct colors, rather than by physically mixing them on a palette.

**ROUGH OR COLD-PRESSED** Paper with a rough surface.

**SABLE** Mink tail hair used to make fine watercolor brushes.

**SGRAFFITO** A technique, usually involving a scalpel or sharp knife, in which dried paint is scraped off the painted surface. Often used for textural effects.

**SHADING** Usually refers to the way areas of shadow are represented in a drawing and is invariably linked with tone.

**SIGHT SIZE** The measurement of the size of a distant object as you see it, which is then transferred exactly to the paper.

**SILVERPOINT** A method of drawing whereby a fine piece of silver is dragged over a piece of prepared paper: Chinese White watercolor provides a matte surface to which the tiny particles of silver adhere.

**SOFT PASTEL** The original and most common form of pastel. The weak solution of gum used in their manufacturing ensures a very soft texture.

**STIPPLING** A method of drawing whereby tiny dots of color are applied close together to create an area of tone.

**SURFACE** The texture of the paper. In Western papers – as opposed to Oriental – the three standard grades of surface are rough, semi-rough (cold pressed or NOT), and smooth (hot-pressed or HP).

**TECHNICAL PEN** A relatively recent innovation in which the tip of the pen is hard and inflexible and designed to give a consistent width of line regardless of the pressure placed on it.

**TONE** The degree of light reflected from a surface.

**VIEWFINDER** Two L-shaped pieces of cardboard that form a framing device. This is usually held at arm's length and the scene to be drawn can be seen through it.

**WASH** A layer of color, often uniform in tone, applied across the paper with a brush.

**WATERCOLOR** A quick-drying paint made from ground pigments and a water-soluble binding medium such as gum arabic. The medium is characterized by its luminosity.

**WAX RESIST** The process by which wax crayons are used to protect areas of the paper when watercolor paint is applied.

**WEIGHT** Watercolor paper is measured in lbs (pounds per ream) or gsm (grams per square meter). It comes in a large range of weights, although the standard machine-made ones are 90 lb (190 gsm), 140 lb (300 gsm), 260 lb (356 gsm) and 300 lb (638 gsm). The heavier papers, 260 lb and over, generally do not need stretching.

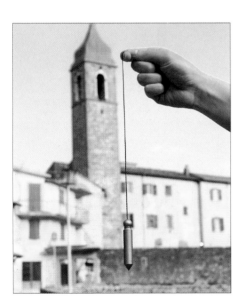

*Plum line*

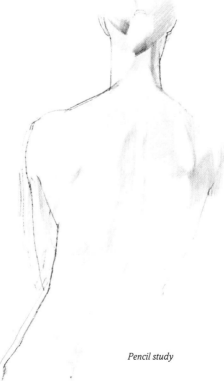

*Pencil study*

---

### A NOTE ON MATERIALS

● Avoid using Chrome colors when you work with watercolor as they carry a significant health risk. There is no danger with any other pigments, provided artists take sensible precautions and avoid licking brushes with paint on them.

● Soft pastels generate a good deal of dust, so it is best to avoid inhaling the pigment powder as much as possible. If you are working indoors, make sure the room is well ventilated.

● The brush sizes given in this book refer to Winsor & Newton brushes. They may vary slightly from those of other manufacturers.

# INDEX

## ACKNOWLEDGMENTS

**Author's acknowledgments**
James Horton would like to thank all the artists who have contributed to this book, especially those who entrusted their drawings into my safekeeping. Thanks also to the photographers at the DK studio whose helpfulness and cheerful nature made every photo session a happy occasion. Particular thanks to Steve Gorton whose patience and professional skill made sure that the location shoot in Tuscany was successful. Thanks also to everyone at DK who worked on the book.

**Picture credits**
Key: t=top, b=bottom, c=center, l=left, r=right, a/w=artworks, RAAL= Royal Academy of Arts Library

Endpapers: Jane Gifford; p2: John Ward, RA, RAAL; pp 6/7: a/w James Horton; p8: t Pontormo, Uffizi, Florence/Ikona; b Holbein, Staatliche Kunstsammlungen Dresden; p 8/9: c Canaletto, Courtauld Institute Galleries; p9: t Breughel, Hamburger Kunsthalle; b Rembrandt, Albertina Graphische Sannlung; p10: t Constable, Victoria and Albert Museum/ Bridgeman Art Library; c Delacroix, Louvre, Paris/ Réunion des Musées Nationaux; p11: t Degas, Tate Gallery, London; bl Van Gogh, Gift of Miss Edith Wetmore, 1960-232-1, Courtesy of Cooper-Hewitt, National Museum of Design, Smithsonian Institution/Art Resource, NY; br Spencer, by courtesy of the National Portrait Gallery, London, © Estate of Stanley Spencer 1994 all rights reserved DACS; p12: Fouquet, New York Metropolitan Museum/ Visual Arts Library; p20: a/w James Horton; p22: t Karen Raney; b Cézanne, Kunsthaus Zurich; p23: t John Ward, RA, RAAL; b Jane Stanton; p26: t Rembrandt, The British Museum; b Karen Raney; p27: t Kay Gallwey; b Percy Horton; p28: t

Jason Bowyer; cl Percy Horton; br Neale Worley; p29: tr William Wood; b Neale Worley; p31: a/w Neale Worley; pp32/33: all James Horton; p34: tr Sue Sareen; c Neale Worley; b Richard Bell; p36: tl Norman Blamey, RA; br James Horton; p37: all Sharon Finmark; p40: Michelangelo, Graphische Sammlung Albertina, Vienna; b Thomas Newbolt; p41: t Paul Lewin; b Donald Hamilton Fraser, RA, RAAL; p42: all James Horton; p 44: a/w James Horton; p48: t Thomas Newbolt; b Jon Harris; p48/49: Boudin, Marmotton Museum/Dorling Kindersley; p49: tr Jane Stanton; c l Anne-Marie Butlin; p54: b Richard Bell; p54/55 Van Dyck, The British Museum; p55: t Percy Horton; b Paul Lewin; p56: a/w James Horton; pp 58/59: all Neale Worley; p60: tl Karen Raney; rest William Wood; p62: tl a/w Richard Bell; p64: t Rubens, The British Museum; b Sue Sareen; p65: t Diana Armfield, RA; b Norman Blamey, RA; p66: a/w James Horton; p68: t John Ward, RA; rest James Horton; p70: bl James Horton.

**Dorling Kindersley would like to thank:** Ruth Kendall for her help and Steve Gorton and his excess baggage for helping to make the Italian photo shoot possible.